Renewing Urban Teaching

Renewing Urban Teaching

L. F. CLAYDON
Senior Lecturer in Education, La Trobe University

With contributions from

MARTA RADO
Centre for the Study of Teaching, La Trobe University

ROD NICHOLLS
Lecturer in the Department of Drama and Communications, Salisbury College of Advanced Education, Adelaide

NICHOLAS SZORENYI-REISCHL
Centre for the Study of Innovation in Education, La Trobe University

CAMBRIDGE
at the University Press
1973

Published by the Syndics of the Cambridge University Press
Bentley House, 200 Euston Road, London NW1 2DB
American Branch: 32 East 57th Street, New York, N.Y.10022
Australian Branches: 296 Beaconsfield Parade, Middle Park, Victoria 3206
184 Sussex Street, Sydney, N.S.W. 2000

Library of Congress Catalogue Card Number: 73-77266

ISBN 0 521 20268 X

Printed in Great Britain by
C. Tinling & Co. Ltd., London and Prescot.

Contents

Acknowledgements

A book such as this inevitably owes a great debt to many people. Prominent among them are the following:

Those of my colleagues who worked with the teams in the schools.

The Principals and Staffs of the schools themselves: the value of their contribution to this venture in teacher education can hardly be over-estimated.

Those gifted and dedicated teachers who, as team members, gave so much time, thought and effort to the schools, to their university studies and to the project *per se*.

Melbourne, 1973   L.F.C.

To
Pat
together with
Matthew, Benedict and Cressida

Preface

In 1971 the School of Education of La Trobe University in Melbourne was in its second year of life. Courses leading to the post-graduate Diploma of Education, the initial qualification for teaching which is awarded by Australian universities, had been established, although they remained subject to constant review and were to undergo considerable modifications in succeeding years. The School was committed to a search for more effective procedures for training and educating teachers and was not deluded that it had achieved any such thing at this early point in its growth. Nevertheless, Diploma courses had been set up and attention must now be turned to the creation of courses leading to advanced qualifications, first among which was to be the degree of Bachelor of Education (B.Ed.), a degree to be gained consequent upon gaining the Diploma of Education. In the main the candidates for the degree would be people with teaching experience and developed specialisms.

The problem of how a staff that was necessarily small at this point of the institution's growth could cater for the entire range of student interests at this level of study had taxed the School from its foundation. Under its Dean, Professor Ronald Goldman, the foundation staff decided to isolate a number of pressing concerns in contemporary education and to found centres for the study of these areas, staffing each with a multi-disciplinary team under a chairman. Courses contributory to the B.Ed. would be developed with reference to the areas with which these centres would be primarily concerned.

The Centres formed were five in number.

Centre for the study of Urban Education
Centre for the study of Innovation in Education
Centre for the study of Comparative Education
Centre for the study of Teaching
Centre for the study of Media and Communication

The staff made their own choices of centre and then turned to the creation of relevant courses.

Although this procedure might be said to fail to cater for all student demands, two things can also be said. First, other universities, including the two in Melbourne besides La Trobe, could be seen to cater for these unmet demands. Secondly, the areas identified by the centre structure at La Trobe were poorly or not at all catered for in Australian universities at the time. More importantly again, the areas of study were such as to serve the cause of equipping or re-equipping the practising teacher for the demands of the late twentieth century. This was a consideration that did not rest upon what other universities were doing but upon what schools needed.

Early in the year the newly created Centre for the study of Urban Education sponsored a course of a special nature which was specifically designed to meet the last mentioned objective. It was given the title, 'City Educational Task Force'. The following is taken from the course description which was circulated to all those who responded to the advertisement for the course.

This is a school based and problem oriented course leading to the award of the degree of Bachelor of Education from La Trobe University.

Selected candidates must accept secondment from their present posts to be placed as a team in a particular inner-city school where they will form part of that school's staff.

Apart from the usual 'free time' allowance to staff, the team will be allowed not less than one fifth of their commitment for special investigation.

The work of the team will have a three fold aspect:
    (a) normal teaching duties subject to the conditions specified above.
    (b) analysis and investigation of problems identified in consultation with the Principal and Staff of the school.
    (c) innovative procedures in respect of the curriculum and organisation of the school.

The aspect of the course described above will have a value of three units from a total of nine required for the successful completion of the course.

In extension and complement to this the selected candidates will take, over the two years' duration of the course, a minimum of six units of study designed to have particular relevance to the team's work in the school.

The central idea of this project was to combine intensive and rigorous teacher education with a definite and practical objective, namely the creation of relevant programmes of education for the city child. Closely allied to this was the intention to study processes of change within particular schools in order to become better informed as to how change is best effected in the real situation of the school.

The first Task Force team was selected in the year mentioned and a second was formed in the following year. The hope is that at least one team will be formed each year and that, as an Educational Task Force (E.T.F.) reaches the end of its life of two years, its members will disperse elsewhere to act as catalysts for change in other schools.

Of the number of university staff who became involved in the project, some were concerned with the teaching of courses of the kind described as complementary in the course description, courses which informed the teams in respect of the problems identified and the innovative initiatives made by them in their schools. Most of these courses were open to any B.Ed. student. However, some of these staff and others beside became attracted to the work to be done in the schools. Together with the director of the project, whose main concern was precisely this work, they brought their own specialisms and interests into conjunction with those of the teams to develop a number of enterprises to meet particular needs within the schools concerned.

The rationale for the project as a whole, the characteristics of the schools who co-operated, the work of the teams together with its effects, and the activities of the university staff who worked with the teams in the schools, make up the substance of this book. Besides the main author, contributions have also been made to the book by the university staff who worked with the teams. It seemed to the main author that it was infinitely preferable that they should speak for themselves rather than have him speak for them. Happily they agreed that this was so. This account is the richer for it.

Since much that follows in this book bears reference to it, a note on 'general studies' as practised in the State of Victoria is perhaps requisite even though to attempt a definition which would secure anything approximating to common acceptance would be a hazardous venture in this or any other context.

In 1968 the then Director of Secondary Education initiated a move towards modes of schooling which accorded more closely with children's learning processes than the centrally inspired and examination oriented curriculum which then prevailed, with its water-tight compartments of traditional academic disciplines and lack of articulation between one compartment and another. One of nine principles promulgated read as follows:

The basic curriculum offered, though it may be open to wide choice within it, should embrace at least the Arts, Social Sciences, Mathematics and Physical Education. It is not supposed, however, that all or any of these need be offered as separate 'disciplines', nor indeed that there must be any fixed patterns within or between schools.

The cognitive processes of children, it was argued, did not accord with subject fragmentation. Learning took place with maximal efficiency in the context of unified experience and was not facilitated by arbitrary divisions into 'English' or 'history'. Better then to think in terms of a thematic approach (e.g. The Sea: Loneliness: Working in a City) and to have teams of teachers approaching the theme from various points of view, taking the cue from the perception of that theme exhibited by the children in a particular school. (The move therefore also involved a welcomed increase in teacher autonomy.)

Plainly more than one classroom organisation can serve the ends proposed but one organisation found immediate favour, namely that of the so called 'open classroom' described in later chapters of this book. The general aim was to facilitate independent enquiry on the part of pupils and to create from a number of teachers a multi-disciplinary resource group in constant touch with the pupils. The argument ran that this was incompatible with a series of enclosed boxes called classrooms, each dominated by a single teacher cut off from his fellows and each of dimensions allowing but a minimum of movement and purposeful social interchange among the children in the class.

There has been constant discussion and exchange of view about both general studies and the open classroom from the time all this was first mooted, not least in issues of the journal *The Secondary Teacher* which celebrated the initiative with a special issue entitled *Three years of Change* (no. 157, July 1970). Articles appearing in it include 'An Approach to General Studies; D. White and E. Wynn, and 'Principles to Practice'; B. Hannan. Subsequent articles in the same journal include ; 'Choice is not Enough'; M. Fallers (February 1971), 'Practical Issues within a General Studies Program'; P. Cole (May 1972), and 'What Should Happen in an Open Classroom?'; R. Barnes (August 1972). Other articles still have argued against general studies altogether. Yet others question the adequacy of the principle cited above, thinking it to uphold an undesirable social status quo rather than rejecting it. Controversy is unavoidable and feelings run deep.

PART 1

Needs and Designs

1. *The dimensions of the problem*

Education for teaching and teacher education

Unless there is a major change in the character of modern society, any halt in the training of people to become teachers or the creation of schools for them to teach in would precipitate a crisis of supply. This remains true however stabilised the society's population or relatively slack the immediate demand for school places.

It is not surprising, therefore, that education for teaching, the preparation of educated people for entry into the teaching profession, has had administrative and economic priority over the years. First, education for all and then an increasing length and complexity of education for all rapidly increased the demand for teachers. There followed the attempt to realise the objective of providing equal opportunity for all in education. The extent to which this can be achieved and the question of whether the enterprise is well conceived is open to debate, but the efforts made have created further demands for teachers. Supply, it has appeared, is perpetually inadequate.

In some countries today the position seems to be changing and the apparatus of initial training for teaching may not have to be geared to a constantly rising demand. In England, for example, the report known as the James Report has stated that; 'the supply of teachers is now increasing so rapidly that it must soon catch up with any likely assessment of future demands'.[1] In that belief the committee responsible for the report is of the opinion that; '. . . the highest priority should be given to the expansion . . . of opportunities for the continued education and training of (existing) teachers.'[2] The intention is to remedy a deficiency that it has never been possible to make good in the past, when resources were swallowed up by the need for teachers while the needs of teachers trailed further behind as the number of teachers increased.

It is easy to see why the committee advanced the new order of priority at this time. 'Education', when taken in the sense of systems of schooling and formal instruction, has long been held to follow rather than to initiate social change.[3] Modern society is characterised by rapid social and technological change a feature of which is the accelerated rate at which knowledge accumulates. As a consequence the term 'knowledge explosion' has been

3

invented, an unfortunate expression in some ways since it suggests a once for all event, a sort of intellectual bang and ensuing cloud of informational dust – mushroom shaped no doubt. A better analogy would be with a rolling avalanche which gathers mass as it proceeds. It is plausible to suggest that more research, more examination of educational issues and more publications about education have appeared in the last few decades than at all other times put together.

Teachers who gained their qualifications some years back and have since been absorbed in the day to day routines of the classroom are generally aware that time has made gaps in their professional education. They resolve to 'catch up a bit' by attending a week-end conference run by the Education Authority, where they hear lectures, witness demonstrations, see films and collect impressive lists of recommended reading. They also exchange notes with people not seen since their days at college or university. They leave at the end more aware of what new there is to be known than knowing.

Far fewer teachers can find the time, opportunity and money to make a more effective assault upon the new knowledge. Those who do succeed seek a course leading to an advanced qualification awarded from a tertiary institution which demands a year's full-time or two to three years part-time study. Dissatisfied with the fractional 'course' and with snatching the occasional hour to read part of a book, they are ready to re-engage themselves in the exacting business of disciplined learning.

The teachers who make this move are generally highly motivated and unusually resilient people of great value to their profession. It is the common experience of lecturers that they are enjoyable to teach, being responsible and demanding in their approach. They possess an eagerness to learn allied to a subscription to the business of teaching that is correspondingly strong but rarely fluffy or romantic.

However, this must not be taken to imply that the teacher who is unexceptional in these attributes is necessarily or usually incapable of benefiting from such endeavours, or that he is entirely unwilling to seek such benefit. As Perry has pointed out, the ordinary teacher is not a dedicated and selfless saint who is vocationally obsessed to the point of self sacrifice,[4] but he is an intelligent human being who is as well disposed to do his work and discharge his responsibilities as his neighbour who conducts a business, works in a bank or manages a store.

Like his neighbour the teacher becomes absorbed in the structure of his day to day life and affairs. He develops a way of doing things as he becomes a seasoned member of his profession and a family man. He adjusts and then stablilises the mode of his adjustment into a life style. In an unpejorative sense of the term he becomes conservative, a fact that McLeish has commented on with special reference to differences in attitude and outlook between students taking initial courses of training and those taking courses some time after qualification.[5]

In the conservative condition, change, innovation and so forth can constitute a challenge which often has the quality of a threat. It is important to take note of this because it implies that innovation is not without hazards. When the highly motivated minority of teachers who become teacher-students and thereby gain a transformed view of schooling return again to their classrooms they may well not make for social comfort, a fact that will receive further examination a little later.

The likelihood that there will be a return has first to be established and it is perfectly reasonable to suppose that such a return is not the final or even the immediate aim of the teacher-student. There is a cynical comment to the effect that success in teaching is to be measured in terms of distance from the classroom.[6] It reflects the fact that promotion in the educational system in many countries either progressively reduces teaching involvement as one moves towards the principalship, or promotes one out of the school altogether into colleges, universities or posts such as inspector and curriculum adviser.

Of course, people already in positions to some degree removed from the classroom normally figure very significantly amongst those who become involved in education as teachers but there is no paradox in talking of the education of people as teachers when their dominant concern is still with teaching and educating. Nevertheless, their number adds to the general picture of a present situation where comparatively few teachers become deeply involved in the thoroughgoing study of education once they achieve qualification as teachers and, of those who do, still fewer remain for long within the general body of the teaching force.

The teacher-student and his teaching role

Suppose that a teacher is enrolled at a university for a course leading to an advanced qualification in education, to be taken part-time over two years. He is accorded a certain relief from teaching duties in the form of study leave which amounts to something like a day 'off' per week. In all other respects he is on a par with his colleagues as he was before enrolling for the course.

Reviewing the general pattern to which this teacher-student is likely to conform we find that he first entered university or college from school, returned again to school as a qualified teacher and now, as one of the minority who take extensive courses, he takes journeys in two directions over the same time-span, going sometimes to the school and the task of teaching and sometimes to the university to study education. The point of interest is that his day to day pre-occupations with the task are but contingently related to his intellectual tussles with Piagetian theory and statistical analysis. In the extreme case the advanced student may pursue his studies in almost conscious distinction from the work he does in his school. Indeed, central to his motivation may be a notion that the qualification he now seeks affords him a ticket of escape from the classroom. In his talk of 'personal development' may be detected an intimation that he requires something as an antidote to the feeling of dead-endedness which oppresses him in his school.

This condition need not be supposed to have general sway. In the normal course of things universities offer learning opportunities in the hope that what is gained will be carried back into schools and classrooms with some excitement, there to be translated into practical outcomes. Similarly, most teacher-students wish to make use of their intellectual gains in the same way and derive pleasure from the prospect.

Let us suppose a particular teacher-student to feel this way. There are things he now sees can be done and he sets about the task of doing them. In the first instance it is a matter of chance whether anyone else in the school notices what he finds it possible to do. Furthermore, it is a matter for speculation whether what he does do is, in fact, an advance upon what is usually done in the school. Assume, however, that it is an advance upon the usual and that his colleagues on the staff do notice that he is making changes. It remains a matter of chance whether the changes are perceived as improvements or whether they are viewed as interesting eccentricities imported from a place untroubled by the practicalities and anxieties of school – this school at any rate.

What the individual post-graduate student gains from his study may therefore remain alarmingly specific to himself and the children he teaches. In addition he may find that he is severely restricted by the organisation of the school which may not accommodate all that he wishes and is able to do given the opportunity. He thus becomes isolated with his new understandings and the latter can be denied a creative practical outcome beyond a certain, possibly very limited, point.

Impediments to change

The report from the Department of Education and Science in England, popularly called the James Report after the Chairman of the committee which produced it, reviews the field of teacher education and advances as a first priority the development of in-service training for existing teachers, advocating that leave for purposes of study should become the rule.[7] It proposes that teachers should be released from duties in school while they study in order to obviate the double loadings so often incurred by taking courses 'part-time'. Secondly it proposes that special personnel, to be called professional tutors, be appointed to serve schools by facilitating study leave for staff and by relating courses taken to the work and needs of the school.[8]

All this and more in the report is very much to the good. It seems abundantly true to say, '. . . no teacher can in a relatively short time, or even in an unrealistically long period at the beginning of his career, be equipped for all the responsibilities he is going to face'.[9] However, the report does not cover all the eventualities of an unfortunate nature that have been outlined in the previous section. Even with the introduction of the professional tutor, the social phenomena within the school which have been mentioned may still have the results described. The report envisages that it will still only be a minority of teachers who will seek courses of an extended and advanced kind from universities. The teacher who does so will stand in a special position within the school and among his fellow teachers, distinguished in part by his readiness to devote time to rigorous study. This is still to take on a task of some magnitude whether under the conditions of an improved future or with things as they are at present. What there is to be known bears no relation to the eight-hour day. But that is but one way to look at it. Whether at present or under conditions proposed by the report, the teacher-student stands in receipt of privilege to some extent in that he has obtained some time off from Johnny and Form Three. As a result he may incur a degree of disapproval or even inspire a certain malignance of attitude among some colleagues, although this does not have to be the case for it be true that his fellow teachers see his position as special nor for the fact to have the effect of dividing him off from the others. That comes about when he seeks to employ his new knowledge in the school.

Once a teacher-student begins to make changes and to depart from the usual way of working it will be recognised that his departures are intended to improve upon the usual. For that reason the changes that he makes, even in the sealed context of his own classroom, are all too simply construed as implying criticism of those who still do the usual thing. Innovations imply negations of the efficacy of the usual.

The tendency in any person once established in an occupation to develop a certain conservatism of approach need not close the mind. It should not be thought that 'giving in' to the tendency blinds the ordinary person to the fact that changes have been recommended or that there are arguments for change. To the contrary, he is likely to be watchfully aware of changes and urgings for change and to be made anxious by them.[10] When this anxiety finds its focus with the teacher-student in the adjacent classroom rather than to be comfortably distant in a university or frozen within the pages of a learned journal, then the work of the teacher-student is the more easily-interpreted as constituting some sort of threat. Certainly it presents an uncomfortable challenge.

Both the teacher-student and the 'ordinary' member of staff whose class-room neighbour he is are members of the loosely knit and sub-sectioned group that is the school's staff. Any group is a conservative agency, protective of its customary ways, which do not consist solely of the policies and the organisa-tion of the school, responsibility for which is ultimately vested in the principal, but are also concerned with how, in that administrative framework, the staff comes to translate policy in terms of common attitudes and approaches. There is a general manner of procedure which unites the staff and the degree of deviance from this group identifying commonality which is considered permissible becomes progressively clearer of definition and limited in scope over time. Schools develop traditions; there is talk of the 'ethos' or 'at-mosphere' of the school. The customary ways of doing things are customary simply because members of the group, particularly the stable and enduring members, subscribe to those ways as valuable above other ways. A new-comer's lack of interest in or disregard of 'how we do things here' is a danger sign, a warning that the cohesiveness of the group may be at risk.

These phenomena of social systems constitute a major hazard in what Sarason calls the obstacle race for innovative proposals which any such proposal must run if it is to achieve implementation.[11] Many fail to complete the course precisely for the reason that conventional ways are not recognised as indicators of the group's value system, the apparent or real flouting of which will bring offence and resistance.

The teacher-student may have considerable autonomy within his own classroom but he is not totally independent. He can be reached and stopped in numerous ways. The case is the more acute when his aim is to secure acceptance and a wider adoption of his procedures.

It must be emphasised here that the reference is to perfectly ordinary people of goodwill; to the sort of person most of us are. It is therefore quite unsatisfactory to rely upon a possiblity that this sort of resistance may not be shown, that it need not be as has been described for the teacher-student. A contingency is not necessarily a rare event; it can be a constant accompani-ment. Although it may not happen it always does just the same. What has been discussed above comes near to falling into this category.

Better then to take Sarason's analysis of the process of innovation seriously rather than to allow romantic optimism to distort one's view of people as they are, a mode of thought which is not entirely absent in the James Report even if it is dispersed amongst a body of otherwise carefully considered analysis. There is no way to evade the inconvenient possibilities that have been discussed here. Most of us have not the unselfish rationality required to seek constantly for that which demonstrates or seeks to persuade us that what we thought to be best, perhaps after careful consideration over years, is merely second best or less. If proposals for change are ineptly introduced then normal conservatism may well calcify into protective and obdurate reaction.

It is not at all clear that the James Report has taken this into consideration. Perhaps it is a separate problem. If that is so it can be argued that the problem has a logical priority over any which is to do with particular innovations if one wishes to create a system of active schools, that is to say a system in which the school is as much the originating point of ideas as it is a reception point for them. This pertains whether we talk of education in England, America, Australia or elsewhere.

The point may be illustrated by reference to the British Schools Council Working Paper entitled 'Cross'd with Adversity'.[12] The thirty-three points summarised in its final chapter are predominantly ones which could only be realised through the work of teachers. There are perhaps some which could be carried through by people coming into the school for a while and concerning themselves exclusively with an action research programme: examples might be work to do with parent participation (Point 23) or the evaluation of the curriculum (Point 12). The paper recognises this but comments that the participation of staff would still be valuable. One may wonder whether any project could be valuable to the school as such in the absence of staff participation, no matter how illuminating the eventual analysis of the data might be. However, many of the recommendations rely directly upon the teachers in the school. Examples are as follows.

Measures to help the disadvantaged pupil should be part of the general educational policy of the school. (Point 1)

Changes in teaching methods, in organisation and in the social function (of the school) are necessary. (Point 2)

(Teachers must become acquainted with) the factors within the home and the community producing social and educational deprivation. (Point 3)

(Teachers should be) ever ready to seize on signs of dormant talent in order to promote a general improvement. (Point 4)

Experimental programmes to explore possibilities should be developed under a more flexible organisation (which is the result of staff planning). (Point 25)

9

Social and cultural deprivation is not the sole problem education today has to face. Too many children who are not disadvantaged in terms of social environment, are not involved in what, to them, is a meaningful experience during the thousands of hours of their school careers. What they fail to learn as a consequence, what they do not find valuable once learned and so reject and forget in a very short time, constitutes a pre-disposing factor contributory to future disadvantage. Thus, if many come to school with disadvantage, many who do not may yet leave school in just such a condition.

For all this to be dealt with an effective teacher-education programme is essential. Through his studies the teacher-student will become increasingly aware of the school malfunction described above. Most teachers are well aware of the obvious symptoms; the bored and disaffected child, the poverty of work produced and the lack of progress made. The teacher-student will have the opportunity to come to grips with causal determinants and the wider effects they have. In this way he will come to see the immediate problems with greater insight and in a wider context.

He will also engage himself in analyses of contemporary innovations in schools which are being mounted in various parts of the world.[13] He will be encouraged to relate this to his own teaching situation and procedures. For the teacher-student the need for change is not now seen as a threat but as a welcome challenge and a stimulus to creative work. This is not always the reality but it is a reasonable hope which must not be dashed by obstructing the way to practical outcomes.

Institutional malfunction

The isolated teacher-student encounters the resistance to change described and analysed earlier. He is supported and encouraged at a distance but still on his own in the practical situation. He must save up his enquiries and uncertainties for next week's seminar or tutorial.

The overall effect of this may be unfortunate in the extreme. Demonstrably urgent problems cry out for the insights which university researchers can provide but their work can be vitiated or restricted once the individual attempts to make use of them; theory moves swiftly on while practice drags its feet and the gap between them widens.

Yet education is a practical activity.[14] The study of Education (capital E), therefore becomes something of a curiosity if it does not inform the task of educating. If one looks at the beginnings of Education as a university study one finds this conception writ large in the work of John Dewey, the principal architect of the introduction. He built into his programme of university

10

studies a functional and ongoing relationship between practical activity within a school and the theoretical studies the student was to pursue. For Dewey the notion of Education without the presence of a task, or the idea of studying teaching in the absence of the taught, was as bizarre as the notion of science without a laboratory.[15] Not everyone would agree with him that the aims and methods of schooling are matters which 'it is the business of philosophy to decide',[16] but few will argue with R. S. Peters when he points out that the concept of education has both a task and an achievement aspect[17]. Omit either aspect and what then results is something other than Education.

At first sight a simple increase in the numbers of teacher-students lends credence to an impression that a powerful research effort into such vital areas as the social and cultural antecedents to educability, the psychological foundations of effective learning and the factors influencing teacher effectiveness, channels directly into the work of schools along a continuum of effort.

What has been examined here produces a different impression. Instead of a continuum there are two discrete elements which stand adjacent to each other. They are intended to be complementary and they can be, but each can stand independently of the other. The more the teacher-student treks now to the university to study Piaget or the Parkway Project and now to the school to deal with Johnny and Form Three the more the reality is separateness, a kind of educational apartheid which vitiates the influence of authoritative research upon practical procedures. The gap between what could be done and what is done threatens to widen.

At best this would all be undesirable but if we are to lend any importance to the work of people such as Illich and Goodman it could be disastrous.[18] The dilemmas of modern society which are the outcomes of rapid social, cultural and technological change, frequently overtake the school and reveal what might be called the pathology of education; what goes on in classrooms becomes out of step with what goes on in the lives of teachers, pupils and parents. Whether in content, interpretation of content or general organisation there is a felt lack of fit, yet, as this becomes an increasing hazard for the school, education is called upon to play an originating part in the amelioration of the defects of change in the larger society; the failure to check poverty, social inequality and social divisions, the lack of satisfaction in work and so on. Failure in these efforts results in children becoming the carriers by whom the very same problems may be projected into the future in severer form. Education may follow social change but the general effort towards change of this nature is now seen to be best effected by casting the school in the role of executive agent.

The series of compensatory programmes and the money provided by government in America, the mounting of Educational Priority Area projects in England, all reflect the urgency of the problems.[19] The James Report underlines the importance and the difficulty of the tasks which must eventually rest upon the shoulders of teachers in school and which have occasioned a great deal of activity in universities all over the world, intended to provide guides and tools for the eventual carriers of the burden. School systems, schools themselves and those engaged in teacher education are inescapably engaged in a running battle to re-align skills and procedures with new knowledge and objectives.

However, these institutions can all too easily act in disassociation from each other. The lack of functional articulation of their various efforts often makes them organisationally spastic. The various departments of the administration, themselves sometimes operating in disregard of other departments,

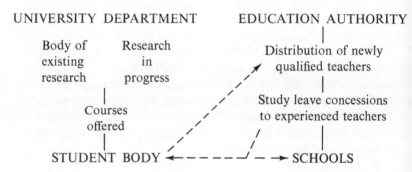

UNIVERSITY DEPARTMENT   EDUCATION AUTHORITY

Body of   Research   Distribution of newly
existing   in   qualified teachers
research   progress

Courses   Study leave concessions
offered   to experienced teachers

STUDENT BODY ← — — — — — ⌐ — → SCHOOLS

issue regulations and make provision through channels which may become as resistant to change as hardened artteries are to the passage of life blood. University departments have their own bureaucracies, nervously vigilant of academic standards and the proper conduct of the pursuit of knowledge. The concept of school as an insulated place, self-contained in all essentials, is still prevalent; it is the same sort of concept as yields the notion of the university as an ivory tower. However much people may protest to the contrary, we have not yet divested ourselves of these concepts; Goodman's talk of 'school monks' and corresponding talk of 'academics' tell the tale.

In far too many areas our various educational institutions do not interact with each other so much as act upon each other rather like marbles in a bag, and where this is so then there is an instance of institutional malfunction. As an example consider how a university department of education typically relates to an Education Authority on the one hand and the schools to which its students will go on the other. The diagram (page 12) over-simplifies perhaps but does not misrepresent the facts.

The relation is maintained only by the movements from one system to another by those who are first students and who might eventually become teacher-students; the systems themselves remain apart. Thus the way in which new knowledge reaches the schools is entirely haphazard and dependent upon the tenacity and wisdom of isolated individuals.

The project to be described here is based upon the argument that the problems facing us can only be resolved by teachers working amongst teachers upon the common ground of the school. New knowledge and skills must be brought to it rather than sent or fetched by messengers in the shape of unsupported persons such as the teacher-student. Relying on teacher-students does not constitute the sort of partnership of function proposed by the James Report. The arena of action must be the school and the nature of the action must be that of conjoint team work by all institutions concerned with schooling.

The organisation necessary to this does not correspond to that represented in the diagram, certainly not in respect of the teacher-student, nor does the James Report's specific recommendations properly mirror its own basic concept. The Educational Task Force project seeks to do this. Designed and implemented under the aegis of the Centre for the study of Urban Education in the School of Education at La Trobe University, of which the project's director was a founder member, it was mounted after a year of planning and negotiation. If it provides some clues for an altered institutional model it will have served its purpose.

2.   The form of the project

A precedent from Chicago

Writing later of his experiences, a former student of John Dewey's named Frederick Smedley commented that the school which was part of the university campus constituted: '. . . a pedagogical laboratory where . . . students (investigate) such questions as the correlation of studies . . . and the adaptation of material . . . to the needs of the pupils'.[1] Students worked in active association with school and university staff. A degree of initiative and responsibility was accorded them. They were not quasi apprentices, hand-held and protected.

Practice schools attached to universities and colleges have long ceased to have the capacity to cope with the mass of students in initial training. In one sense that is probably as well. Such schools were special places whose ethos and conditions of work were often unilluminative of the conditions which the student would encounter once he went his way to unknown schools standing in no such special relation to a university or college.

On the other hand the depth of study, continuity of observation and contact which such schools allowed for, can hardly be counted as well lost. And, in the main, it has been lost. Today's student in initial training is normally placed in a school within the area for a period of time to do his teaching practice. Tertiary staff often visit the school for an hour or so beforehand in order to make arrangements. They make similar occasional visits to 'supervise' the student, remaining with him over the course of a lesson or so and discussing what he did with him afterwards. There are many schools and many students. It is difficult to do more and cover all the students in all the schools.

For the teacher-student as opposed to the student-teacher even this does not occur. No within school liaison occurs at all. This is likely to be the truer in respect of the part-time teacher-student. By the argument of the previous chapter the lack is a most unfortunate one.

Both in respect of the student-teacher and of the teacher-student there have been moves to use the schools of the area in a manner nearer to Dewey's ideas. Fittingly enough one such move has been made by the University of Chicago. Its inspiration was a paper by J. W. Getzels which

14

was published in 1967.[2] With equal fittingness his paper contains a quote from Dewey at an early point in its argument, to the effect that sound theory is 'the most practical of all things'. Getzels' intent is to present a practical proposal that is consistent with the theoretical framework he feels to be proper to an articulated system of education. In effect this amounts to making use of the ordinary school to the same intensive and continuous extent that was possible in the campus school.

Getzels states that:

The hope would be that the school, would become a meeting place of university faculty and school personnel and of parents and other community agents ... It is perhaps time not only for the school to come to the university but for the university to come to the school.[3]

He contrasts what he has in mind with the usual situation to be found at present. His description of the latter has all the characteristics described in the previous chapter as indicative of institutional malfunction.

To be sure there are conferences and workshops in which school people, personnel from other related agencies and sometimes even parents come to the university. But these are artificial meeting grounds ... Sometimes university people come to the school as 'consultants' or to 'do a survey'. These are even less functional, for the university people come as outsiders ... with all the blocks to communication and co-operation that such conditions impose.[4]

It is interesting here to take note of the difference of emphasis between these comments and some remarks on what appears to be an almost identical theme made in the James Report.

It has been suggested by a few witnesses that (university departments of Education) should cease to be involved in the initial training of teachers ... We emphatically reject this ... The U.D.Es should continue to pursue fundamental research and advanced study ... (T)his work obviously benefits from being carried out in a university setting. (However) an active university department will have close relationships with schools ...

It seems possible to argue that the tenor of this passage reveals a possibility that, by this report, the universities will stand in the relationship that Getzels wishes them to alter. It is to be noted that the report states that: 'It is obvious that of all the institutions concerned the Colleges of Education (that is to say not the universities) would be most affected by the proposals of this report.'[5]
It goes on to say that colleges would 'form a new and closer relationship with schools' (page 65). The point to be made is simply that 'closer' is restricted to institutions other than universities.

In his paper Getzels makes much of the fact that, when the new teacher has his first encounter with the school to which he has been appointed, including the school most in need of innovation, he does so as an isolated individual and on the first day of the term. Getzels suggests that the encounter frequently brings 'dismay, discouragement, loss of confidence'. The result is often a retreat from the 'difficult' school or from teaching altogether.

Here the later publication, the James Report, is in closer accord with Getzels. It contains the following recommendation.

We have been told that it is possible for a young teacher to arrive at his school at the beginning of term not only without having visited it to meet the children who will be in his care but without having met the head teacher. (page 36) . . .In the placing of new teachers, particular care should be taken to match them to the schools in which they will start teaching and practising teachers (especially the heads of the schools concerned) should be involved in the process. (page 112).

Getzels suggests that student-teachers should be formed into teams or cadres. The cadre is to be formed during the period of education for teaching but it is to remain intact as a group for at least a year after teaching qualifications have been gained, working as a group within the same school which housed it during the university course. He further suggests that a cadre should comprise a role set, that is to say that its members should represent the various functions of school personnel (e.g. teachers, counsellors psychologists and administrators). All members should receive a training in common, for when they are trained separately 'it is difficult to imagine a program . . . that makes less provision for . . . co-operation'.

Again there are points of accord in the James Report. However, in this case particularly, the report is by no means as specific in its recommendations as to procedures nor is it quite clear that precisely the same conception occurred to the committee. Of course a differentiation of function is more the rule in American schools than in English ones. For example the number of English schools that have counsellors or psychologists as part of the staff is comparatively small.

By Getzels account, then, members of a cadre should be people who have made a conscious choice of the particular school situation in which the cadre is to work. In this instance it is the inner city school as opposed to the more comfortable situation of the outer suburban school. Further to this members of the cadre should be prepared to commit thenselves to a particular school in that category and to work with that school's problems and needs as its point of reference. Getzels contends that; '. . . the problems of the inner city school will not be solved by merely providing training at the university'.[6] He argues further that it is a fundamental error to conceive of the social system of the inner city school as more or less similar to that of the outlying middle-class suburb. He does not say that the latter is quite devoid of problems but that, besides being less severe, the problems are different in kind from those of the inner city school.

The American scene is, of course, a little different from say, the English or Australian situations. The inner city problem in America is compounded by a degree of alienation and a complex of stark ethnic hostilities that is greater than in many other modern societies. Poverty and hopelessness intensify these phenomena. At the same time the locus of the problem is tight drawn about the inner city where, in other countries, it is more diffuse. But none of this prejudices the point that Getzels makes. We may take 'inner city' to be a generic term rather than a geographical description, or we may abandon the term altogether and talk instead of the proportion of disadvantaged children in *any* school.

Concerning his proposal Getzels makes the general comment; 'As far as I know, no current educational institution fills ... the need (for the school to become the meeting place of university, school staff, parents etc.).' He recognised, in 1967, that implementing the suggestion would pose administrative problems but he declares his conviction that it is time; 'to cease letting problems of expediency outweight issues of principle (when) the problems are not insurmountable'. Essentially the principle concerned is as Getzels gave it in a speech in the same year.

... if the school is to function properly there must be communication between those who train the educational personnel, those who utilize the personnel, and those who are served by the personnel. That is, there must be ... interaction between the school, the community and the university.

In 1968 the Department and Graduate School of Education of the University of Chicago gained funds from the Ford Foundation and proceeded to put Getzels' idea into practice. The Education Authority was approached to secure its co-operation and the first cadre was placed in a school. Since that time more cadres have been formed and placed. An extensive programme of evaluation has begun to operate as the first cadre nears the end of its scheduled life.

The project is ambitious and expensive. The report of the Department for 1971 instances many indications that it is achieving positive results.[8] It also notes the interest the project has aroused. The cadre system was then under consideration for adoption in four different parts of the U.S.A. At least one other university had actually made application for funds to implement a similar project.

In the light of the previous chapter one fact still remains. In the Chicago project the cadre members are predominantly new entrants to the profession of teaching. Although they are placed in a school as a group, thus providing a possibility of mutual support, and although there is a continuing association with university staff over an extended period within the school, the problem of the new teacher as an innovating influence which has been discussed in the first chapter must, to some extent, still persist. It is true that the project's first aim was to secure teachers for schools which are usually avoided, but it is also true that these are the schools which stand in need of innovation more than most and that the cadre members were seen as able to effect this. The problem of the new teacher still remains therefore. For example, one of the cadres was considerably affected by the fact that two of its members proved to be incompetent as teachers.[9] As was contended in the first chapter, the possibility that this might prove to be the case is something that *any* new teacher has to live through. While doing so he is, quite sensibly, reluctant to 'chance his arm'.

Modifications and adaptations for La Trobe

The Chicago reports are refreshingly frank about the way in which Getzels' prophecy that difficulties were to be expected was confirmed. In a joint article by the Director of the Project and its Director of Research the comment is made that; '. . . in terms of building unified cadres, in only one of the three (earliest) cases were there marked successes'.[10] It is plausible to suggest that one contribution to these setbacks was the inexperience of the cadres.

The project given the name 'Educational Task Force' was conceived at La Trobe School of Education independently of the developments at Chicago, although the latter furnished an invaluable guide at a subsequent stage. From the outset it was thought to be inadvisable to make use of student-teachers as an innovative instrument. It is therefore the more interesting that later documents from Chicago make mention of the creation of experienced cadres as a desirable extension of the initial plan. This development appears to recognise the necessity to draw a careful distinction between what the two kinds of teacher group – experienced and inexperienced – should have as functions.

The general development of La Trobe's School of Education provided important insights into the distinction. So far as the student-teacher was concerned the School developed an organisation of student experience which is closely in accord with Getzels' central ideas. For the post-graduate Diploma in Education, which is the initial qualification for teaching given in Australian universities, students may opt to join one of five courses, each of which is served by a multi-disciplinary team of staff, and each of which develops its own way of working according to a general brief common to all. In this way relatively small groups of students (e.g. some fifty to seventy) are in association with a stable group of staff, all of whom are well known after a very short time.

The basic learning group is the seminar of between seven to fifteen students. The reference point for course content and seminar discussion is the school. Students in small groups are placed in particular schools in which they work with established teachers for some two days each week over a period of at least one term. In many instances seminars and tutorials are taken in the school itself, with university tutors conducting them jointly with members of the school staff.

Regular meetings of the whole course group are held. In this way the differences between school and school can be examined and explained. It also allows for the airing of common problems and anxieties and for suggestions as to course content and construction to be discussed.

The Educational Task Force project was conceived as a manner of providing particular schools with a specialised resource capable of generating and implementing innovative procedures. It was to do this in part by mounting the 'tailor made' courses of an advanced nature mentioned in the course description. The emphasis was to be on service to the school over a protracted period of time. For all the reasons advanced earlier it seemed obvious that this function was suited to teacher-students rather than to student-teachers. The function supposes competences to be augmented rather than competences to be acquired.

One would hope that many of the graduating teachers of the School would make admirable material for Task Forces in the future. The form of their initial training is such that it should familarise them with the sort of situation that is basic to the Task Force's function. The Task Force is, in fact, a logical extension of the School's concept of education for teaching. If the one is right then the other is. This complementary nature of the School's student-teacher programmes and the Task Force form of teacher-student education was demonstrated by the way in which some of the recipients of the former came into fruitful and active association with one of the Task Force teams with mutual benefit to both groups. This will be discussed a little later.

Further pointers for the project

The Chicago system of cadres is the most fully developed and the closest precedent for the Task Force Project. It has a full documentation in the shape of internal or privately circulated papers which the University of Chicago Department of Education was kind enough to make available to us.

Although it is probable that Getzels was correct in his assertion of 1967 that no current educational institution was working towards the sort of system that the Chicago School of Education has now put into action, there are indications that the shape of teacher-education programmes will change in ways closely in accord with the thinking behind the Chicago project. In England, for example, the University of Bristol has developed its Hillview Project and in the opening chapter of their account of this work Hannam *et al.* make the following comment.

At present the student finds himself placed in a school where he is expected, and expects himself, to operate effectively with neither the experience nor the means to do so. The student in school is typically the 'marginal man' . . . Part of the difficulty is that the proper relations between school and teacher-training institution have never satisfactorily been worked out.[11]

The student mentioned here is the student-teacher and not the teacher-student and the concern is much the same as the Chicago concern, namely how best to equip and to orientate the new professional to the problems of the school which houses the average child, among whose ranks will be found those for whom the traditional school holds little or no significance, relevance or promise of reward. Part of this orientation is not a function of the newcomer but of the school into which he comes and the colleagues he now joins. In their book about the Hillview Project the team of university staff who mounted it clearly identify the factor of group conservatism as it operates to discourage new approaches to teaching.

Other similar ventures in teacher-education are undoubtedly being developed in various parts of the world. But it would be inaccurate to suggest that there have been no antecedents to all this prior to these last few years, whether in America or elsewhere. Most of them have been largely exploratory and severely limited in 'scope. They were largely involved in schemes of initial training rather than to do with the education of teachers, the teacher-student, and generally operated within relatively brief periods of school-based learning focussed upon school based problems. ('School based problems' may be taken to indicate either or both of two closely similar things: (i) the problems of a particular school; (ii) general educational problems as they are manifested within a specific school.)

It is perhaps a little invidious to single out examples of these unsung ventures, yet to do so is a valuable way to trace the development of an idea. It should be understood that what is now cited is not representative of the best that has been done. The instances provided are those in which the author was actively involved in one capacity or another and so can vouch for the accuracy of the account.

Some years before 1967, the Coventry College of Education in England placed a group of students in a particular city high school for a period of six months.[12] During this time the team assumed responsibility for the majority of the curriculum in respect of two classes of children, and almost total responsibility for developing a curriculum change in the areas of geography, history and English.

Over the six months this small group of final year students, in association with subject teachers of the school and two college staff, developed a programme of environmental studies designed to suit the learning character-istics and the cultural understandings of the pupil population concerned. They made a film of the work as it developed. It was still being shown to students some years later, both in Coventry and elsewhere.

The school in which this took place was under sentence of death. A new comprehensive school was in the final stages of completion half a mile away. It had opened its doors two years before, gradually increasing its intake as its various stages of construction were accomplished. The intake of the school where the student team did its work became more and more of an 'overspill', a euphemistic term for a collection of unselected children. Not surprisingly the morale of the staff was low. Few of them would obtain posts in the compre-hensive school upon the final closure of their present school. The Local Authority was naturally reluctant to do much for the doomed premises beyond that which was absolutely necessary for minimal efficiency and safety. The children were themselves perfectly aware of the fact that they were there simply because the comprehensive 'didn't want us'. The same realisation possessed their parents. All in all it was an unpromising climate for aspiring teachers and *their* teachers to enter with a view to implementing new ideas.

Yet it was undeniably the case that the period of six months produced a quite marked change and increase of competence in these 'selected out' children of the inner city. Secondly, the same sort of gain was clearly evident in the teaching performances of the student team. More important still, the students became fiercely attached to the children they taught and who, at the outset, had given more than a fair share of trouble. They were undemonstra-tive in their approach; nothing that smacked of possessive protection or cloying charity. They had simply come to value the children as persons and to see their task as facilitating their growth as such.

It was also noticeable that the degree of feed-back and dialogue from the staff grew dramatically over the period. This was something of a surprise.

Initially the staff retreated gladly to the staffroom in gratitude for being 'let off'. With the school in the painful situation that has been described one could have expected that the resistance of group conservatism would have been allied to apathy, and that little interaction above the necessary would result. Indeed this was precisely what individual students who had previously been placed in the school for their practice period had found. As a consequence the school had come to be used as little as possible for teaching practice. But, as with the children themselves, the cure for inertia does not consist of action which appears to confirm the appropriateness of the selecting out process and, by the same token, to insulate the student-teacher from the sort of situation which confronted the team is no way of equipping him to survive and combat it.

Much later, this time in Edge Hill College of Education in Lancashire, the opportunity was presented to repeat the procedure. By that time the Liverpool Education Priority Area project had been mounted and was making use of students from the college for work in particular schools in the city. The Plowden Report's concept of positive discrimination was being put to work.[13] Not only by an infusion of funds for the material upgrading of downtown schools but by positive practical participation in the instructional programme within the schools by educationists and students, the effort was to instill confidence and a sense of worth into children, staff and parents.

But not all schools with problems lie in the decayed centres of cities. One rural school not far from the college made known its severe staffing and other problems and requested the college to assist. To be brief, the request was met in much the way that the work in Coventry had suggested and it secured much the same result. However, this time, precisely as in the Chicago experience in respect of one cadre (see page 18) the team of students developed a functional limp which constantly threatened the enterprise. Not all the students were competent enough to carry through the work. In addition the resistance of staff conservatism was much more evident and intractable, a fact that sapped the team's confidence and, in particular, that of the less competent of their number. Yet there remained the fact that the same sort of gain was made as in the Coventry 'experiment'.

Ruling considerations and preliminary steps at La Trobe

Participation in all the undertakings mentioned in the previous section convinced the director of the Task Force Project of La Trobe University School of Education of the following points, most of which have been discussed earlier but are worth re-identification at this point.

Whether in Chicago, Coventry or Melbourne, America, England or Australia:

(A) If there is to be a positive innovative contribution brought to a school then it must be affected at the hands of established professionals in working contact with staff from universities or other institutions, not the other way round.

(B) There must be a team rather than an isolated individual.

(C) The more fragmented or episodic the contact between team and school staff, team and university resource, university resource and school staff, the less effective the innovative contribution will be and the more the school will be better off relying entirely upon its own initiatives.

(D) The more the interaction between team and university resource is removed from the school and complementary interaction with the staff, the less effective the team will be.

(E) Blessedly, teachers are normal people. Group conservatism of customary ways is to be expected, respected and endured. For this reason a team with an innovative function is unlikely to achieve very much in a relatively short time. Its first tasks are to understand the social system of the particular school, to gain acceptance within it, and to know how it can be utilised to bring about change. Only then may one hope for constructive changes. In the light of this six months is a very short time and a year a relatively short time.

(F) The concern must be for the school and not with innovation *per se*. The concern must be for the school and not for the team *per se*. Innovation must be a consequence of the problems presenting themselves whether these are brought to the staff by the team or vice-versa.

With these general guidelines we were ready to set up the first Educational Task Force. We had first to secure the approval of the scheme by the Victorian Education Department. A degree of special arrangement was required if one was to secure that selected candidates could be seconded as a group to the particular school to be involved. Consultations were arranged with the Director General and Assistant Director General. A series of meetings with the Director of Secondary Education then followed. These subsequently developed into a working partnership which continues to grow. Once persuaded of the probable value of the project all these authorities gave co-operation and guidance.

There is a point worthy of emphasis here. One argument to explain the dichotomy between research and theory on the one hand and classroom practice on the other, places the onus upon the school system and its bureaucratic machinery rather than upon any characteristics of teachers as a

23

group or schools as social systems. It is frequently true that administration deserves criticism of the severest kind. It is often ridiculously rigid in its application of rules and regulations. It is reluctant to sanction the most innocuous of departures from the existing pattern, particularly if this involves spending even a very little more money. It is over-anxious that some sort of precedent could be established which may – just may – open the way for numerous other claims upon it.

Nevertheless the effort must always be to establish a dialogue and then to move towards a dynamic tri-partite enterprise in which school, university resource and administration co-operate. The hope must always be that each partner will not obstruct the other nor allow caution to calcify into blind reaction and then stubborn dogmatism. The testimony from Chicago and the existence of Educational Priority Areas in England contradict any assertion that the hope is vain. Of course the Chicago project is supported by a large grant from the Ford Foundation and the Educational Priority Areas are governmentally inspired in large part. Both therefore enjoy a privileged status. The La Trobe Project did not have this advantage and for this reason could not make the Educational Task Force teams supernumerary to the staff of the school. Their share of normal teaching duties was not always to the good of the work they were intended to do. Certainly they could have done with more time for their innovative and evaluative functions than was granted them by the usual 'time off' entitlement restricted to those with service enough to qualify for it upon enrolment for a university course. One could criticise the Department for not making a special provision in this case.

On the other hand the teacher supply position in Victoria was not good during this period, whatever the English prognostications from the James Report. Many schools suffered difficulty through staff shortage. From the point of view of the administrator it is debatable whether sponsorship of a new project which would be best served by providing supernumerary teachers should take priority over the needs of schools lacking staff. Since it is true that, at this same period, relations between the teachers' organisations and the Education Department were anything but harmonious, it would have been a brave decision to make even if it was undeniably the best one. When there is clear room for argument about the last proposition blame should not be lightly laid.

At about the same time as the consultations with the Education Department were begun, the first public discussions of the Educational Task Force took place. Its director was asked to outline the project to a meeting of Victorian Institute of Educational Research. By the end of the evening it was clear that there would be no question as to whether there would be schools ready to extend an invitation for an Educational Task Force to work in them. Subsequent talks to other bodies whose membership included school personnel confirmed this.

The limitations imposed upon the project by the absence of special funding, together with what seemed due prudence, led to the decision that but one Educational Task Force would be created in each of the first two years. The school receiving the Educational Task Force team in the first year will be referred to as School A, the school receiving a team in the subsequent year as School B. The two schools were selected from those who extended invitations after the first public discussion of the project. Planning in respect of School B therefore took place over a longer period, allowed for more extensive consultation with the principal and staff, and benefited from the fact that much was learned from the first Educational Task Force and its experience.

Life of an Educational Task Force team

From what was said in the immediately preceding section it is clear that it would not have done to think of 'touring' one team around a number of schools for successive periods of, say, six months. Implementation of innovative proposals must run the obstacle race described by Sarason.[14] Haste at the outset may be fatal. Careful preparation must be followed by controlled procedure. Time is needed.

Social process must be allowed to take its own time also. In a broad sense of the term, any aggregate of people put together in a common situation may be said to constitute a group but when six or seven people are selected to form a team the only common reference may be the prospective task. Missing at the initial stage, assuming no prior acquaintance between those now grouped, is any network of relationships between them. There is an absence of shared interests and aspirations at this point.

Joining a school staff as one of a team of seconded teachers further complicates the matter because each member has more than one social and professional task to surmount. He must find a role within the team and participate in its effort to establish an identity with the rest of the school staff, but as an individual he must also achieve his own personal orientation within the social structure of the school and establish his own personal relationships with individual members of staff.

It was planned that a team would meet together as a group several times before moving into the school as an Educational Task Force. At some of these meetings it was planned that a number of school staff would be present and liberal time allowed for informal interaction. It was also hoped that a team would attend staff meetings in the school to assist integration. From the outset there was total agreement with Getzels when he stresses the absurdity of allowing people intended to work closely together only to come into contact with each other on the first day of the working year.

However, it requires the most propitious of circumstances before what is possible prior to the actual event can be more than a breaking of the ice. The main process of social integration can only begin in earnest in the working situation. In the Chicago project the circumstances were propitious and the cadres could be drawn together for a period before they went into the school, during which they were able to get to know each other and to discuss the characteristics of the school where they were to work.

It is regrettable that, in most school systems, very little thought is given to facilitation of the process of integration and role identification. It must go on willy-nilly at the very time that the school and staff are pre-occupied with the new intake of students, the re-arranged time-table, the fresh line-up of classes and many other things. At the risk of labouring the point it is to be pointed out that social networks in a complicated social structure do not run smoothly of necessity. Conflicts of interest and attitude, inaccurate first impressions and much else, prevent it.

Taking all this together it became clear that the Educational Task Force project would be ill served unless the teams were to remain in their respective schools for a period at least as long as the minimum time set for the completion of the general run of B.Ed. courses (The La Trobe B.Ed. is a 'second' degree.) We also bore in mind that the task of evaluation was a component of the scheme. Without knowing how fully or how well a team would accomplish this task it seemed only sensible to accord it time enough to work to avoid such criticisms as: 'The research evaluation of any programme, requires precise description of the educational experiences involved ... Most of the studies here reviewed do not satisfy this requirement.'[15] Hence it was specified that the period of secondment to the school was to coincide with the total duration of the course.

It could be said that, in comparison with the Chicago project, this constituted something of a gain. The cadres continue to work as groups in the school where they are placed for one year after graduation. But they are still 'the new teachers' as it were. Their years in the school prior to graduation must obviously do much to mitigate the temptation within the school to class them as untried fledglings, but there is some difference between this and a situation in which a school receives a group of carefully selected and well tried professionals whose members bring a range of successful experience to their present task.

Assessment of the project: preliminary worries

Our principal question was whether or not the Educational Task Force in a school could effect innovative procedures and undertake evaluative tasks in more effective ways than the isolated teacher in the school. We also wished to know what sort of person would be attracted to the form of course offered by the project and whether the characteristics of those finally selected would show some sort of pattern of common features. A third concern was the way in which particular schools may reveal characteristics peculiar to themselves. All this would require careful case studies of the two teams.

Our belief was that Getzels would prove to be correct in his assertion that schools in particular situations exhibit particular characteristics. But we also believed that his point could be enlarged. The social system of one school differs from that of *any* other school in important respects. To control too much at the outset, or to provide too precise a brief for the Educational Task Force would be to run the risk of obscuring this possibility. Each Educational Task Force must take the school as it was. We felt it to be important not to predispose them to particular ends from without the school.

On the other hand the project sought to investigate ways in which a functional relationship could be established between the university and the school, the focus of attention being the problems and the concerns of the school. The Chicago Project documents indicate that it was soon discovered essential to have a 'liaison person' who would maintain and service such a relationship. The director of the Educational Task Force project incorporated this role into his work. Providing that the relationship was secured and maintained it seemed to be reasonable to suppose that the university staff could as well make innovative proposals as the team or the staff itself.

A further and very important question that would be our concern was to do with the efficacy of the course. The intention was that the experience of the Educational Task Forces would be unlike the possible experience of the individual teacher-student. The latter may feel that his work and the course of study he pursued at the university were not related in fact even though they were intended to be in principle.

We were aware from the outset that there are objections to this way of working which could be made by the methodological purist, to whom 'action research' or 'development projects' are to be viewed with some suspicion at best. Given one frame of reference we tend to agree. However we would suggest that more than one frame of reference may be employed with profit. We recognise that there must be rigorously controlled and methodologically sound investigations if the continuum we have spoken of is to possess any certainty or universality of finding.

But it is a matter of one thing at a time. Allport, in his discussion of eclecticism in psychology makes the point that: '. . . theories that don't work in practical life cannot be entirely sound'.[16] We wanted to see what happened; what worked and what did not. This was the first step. Later, perhaps, we could construct hypotheses about how what happened and what worked came to happen and to work.[17]

The account here given is concerned more with observed processes of change than with outcomes *per se*. It may be a considerable time before any definitive assessment of the worth of the project can be made, but much can be said at this time about the creation of the teams, their introduction into two different schools and their subsequent experiences and achievements.

In comparing school with school, team with team, teacher with teacher and so on, tact may war with truth. Arrogance of judgement can masquerade as accuracy. Comparisons are necessary if one is to understand how conditions affect cases. Where comparisons are made it is only for that reason. We can but report as faithfully as we know how, eschewing the fairy tale on the one hand and the horror story on the other.

3. School needs

School A

The district served by School A is one of a ring of suburbs adjoining the centre of the city. Like so many cities in the modern world, Melbourne's pattern of growth has left such areas in a state of progressive decay. Over a period of years successive migrations to the outer suburbs have denuded them of their more affluent and socially stable residents. These people have been replaced by newcomers who were, in the main, less stable and socially effective than the general run of remaining residents.

Each cycle of this kind therefore tends to depress the economic and cultural potential of the neighbourhood until it eventually takes on a quite different character and reputation from that which it once possessed. Physical change in the district tends to fix the new identity. As private housing declines in resale or rental value with each migration to the outer suburbs, it also declines in state of upkeep until disrepair reaches an extreme point.

At this point it is frequently the case that public authority institutes the process of urban renewal and this was the case with the district in which School A is situated. High-rise flats were built by the Housing Department. Where there were once private houses and gardens there are now car parks and public recreation spaces.

However well planned and desirable this may be once the neighbourhood has become subject to the decline just described, redevelopment of this nature confirms the alteration of the area's character. Public housing tends to increase population density. The area can now support more commercial development in the shape of retail shops, service stations and so forth.

In Australia there is a long established tradition of home ownership. Those who possibly can have sought to own the houses in which they live. Successive economic crises of one sort and another are weakening this tradition but it is still the case that the ordinary Australian thinks of rented accommodation as second best and of public housing as yet further removed from the most desirable residential circumstance. Necessity rather than choice will therefore bring him to School A's area. By the same token the Australian immigration policy assists many thousands of people from selected areas of the world to settle in Australia. Many could not have paid their own passages and, after their sojourn in the hostel accommodation provided for the first few months after arrival, many still cannot afford home purchase. Alternatively they are loth to expend limited capital until a later time.

The pattern of immigration has changed. Initially the principal source was the United Kingdom but, from the late thirties, this predominantly British inflow was joined by other northern Europeans, notably the Germans and the Dutch. Developments in the 1950s saw a continuation of the trend away from the British. Central and then southern European immigrants made up an increasing number of the total immigrant flow. As in the case of the Germans and Dutch, the early arrivals came unassisted. When assisted passage schemes were extended to these countries the number increased substantially. One research worker has pointed out that:

About eighty per cent of Melbourne's migrant Greeks arrived within the last twenty years. By giving assisted passages to several thousand Greek males and heads of families, new and large migration chains were initiated. Earlier Greek migration chains . . . were few and small.[1]

What is true for the Greeks is true also for Italians and of other peoples in the Mediterranean socio-cultural area. By the middle sixties that region had become a very important source of immigrants to Australia.[2] But where the immigrant from northern Europe tends to possess an education and level of skill somewhat superior to that of the average Australian the reverse has proven to be true of the immigrant chains from southern Europe. The change is worthy of note as a wealth of documentation, particularly from the United States of America, indicates. Unless care is taken the flow of immigration may result in the creation of a social category now given the title of 'underclass'.[3] Low potential in terms of educational levels and job capability in the first generation of immigrants tends to settle them at the foot of the social and economic scale and to keep them there until it becomes extremely difficult for succeeding generations to break out of what becomes an underprivileged position. It is no more than an historical accident that the United States has furnished tragic object lessons to the effect that such a condition may be socially explosive as well as morally indefensible. The lessons must be heeded if Australia, Britain or any other developed society is not to develop its own underclass ready to subvert the social structure.

Level of education and economic potentiality apart, the cultural differences between the Mediterranean immigrant and the native Australian are perhaps more marked than between northern European and Australian. It is therefore easier for the Greek or Italian (particularly the mother of the family when confined to the home) to experience a sense of alienation and a consequent need for the support of the familiar. These ethnic groups therefore tend to concentrate in particular areas rather than disperse throughout the city's residential districts. Both economically and culturally they find much more support among their own (ethnic) kind in their new country, Australia. As Tsounis remarks;

Melbourne's Greeks are in the lower range of the socio-economic ladder alongside other immigrants and working classes . . . Just as the response by Greek immigrants to the unequal economic contest is to work hard and long hours and establish their own business, their response to a different social environment is to create one of their own . . . Their response is not new or strange when one considers the great cultural barrier between immigrant and native . . . especially the linguistic barrier.[4]

It is also obvious why they should be found in areas such as that in which School A was situated (and School B for that matter, as we shall later see). In a significant proportion of cases the economic potential of the southern European immigrant more or less pre-selects settlement in an area of public housing or low rental property.

School A began as a High School for Girls. It was built at the start of the century. For many years it served a more or less homogeneous and settled population until the area became subject to the determinants of urban change that have been discussed, when it went through the gamut of changing identities and, over a small span of years, the school served a continually altering population. From being relatively stable and secure economically, the area became one which was increasingly less stable and secure and possessed of a wide range of cultural diversity. Eventually it stabilised once more but at a level considerably below that which previously pertained. The high-rise flats were built. The process of urban renewal was instituted. At the same time the area became increasingly saturated with Mediterranean immigrants so that the school population became predominantly composed of children with parents who were not native Australians. The first language of both the parent and the child was not English and, frequently, the only language of the parent remained that of the country of origin. This was rarely the case with any but the very recently arrived of the children but what was often true was that the child spoke fluently in English whilst being considerably less able to write and sometimes to read English.

Over the same period, pressure for school places in the district became increasingly severe. There had been but small co-ordination of school accommodation with developments in public housing so that this outcome was all but inevitable as more children moved into and then through the school system. To equalise the degree of overstrain across the available school accommodation it became necessary to redistribute the child population in the schools. School A was therefore redesignated as a co-educational school. Though this was not a bad thing in itself it was a further change to which adjustment must be made. In this case it had to be achieved in the absence of a corresponding planned adjustment of staff to match the translation from single sex to co-educational schooling. An almost totally female staff with experience of a girl's school faced a situation where the balance of the sexes became progressively more even.

School A's building was of an old design taken from the English Board Schools of the 1890s. As the student population continued to grow the building became dramatically inadequate. Difficulties unconnected with over-crowding also multiplied, including that of the child whose English was confined almost completely to the spoken word. Staff were not attracted to the situation and left almost as fast as they came.

It was inescapable that School A, must have a new building. At the urging of an enlightened Director of Education the construction sanctioned was of a design which accorded with contemporary educational needs extending beyond the relatively simple requirement for floor space. It was not to echo again the philosophy underpinning the design of the first building for School A and that of the primary schools about it, namely that of the English Education Act of 1870 which sanctioned building when it was necessary to 'fill up gaps' left by voluntary agencies and their educational establishments. What was now proposed consisted of a community complex. It was to include school provision over the range of schooling, a library, and public meeting places.

The suggestion was approved by State Parliament. The long business of drawing up specifications, scheduling phases of construction and assessing cost limits was begun. After some two years the work was complete. It is again to the credit of the now retired Director of Education that it was carried through in close co-operation with parent organisations, professional partici-pation from the teachers and with the local council. The response from the first named of these was particularly eager and particularly important, if only for the reason that the opportunity did much to indicate that the Mediterranean migrant was not to be regarded as a 'foreign' accretion whose proper concerns did not include the working of Australian institutions beyond the point of benefiting or suffering from them.

The design of the high school accommodation in the new complex is informed by a modern concept of schooling. It is not thought of as a place suited to a system of collective instruction in which the teacher instructs a passive audience in those things which are for its own good but none of its origination. Instead it tries to provide an environment wherein the individual student may seek learning experiences at the spur of his own interests and over the range of intellectual, social and emotional development. He will thus interact freely with the teacher in terms of his own awakening (and awakened) interests and activities. The teacher will interpret and guide rather than direct and pontificate. The student's sense of personal responsibility and his impulse to learn are thus immeasurably strengthened. He is now part of a joint enterprise rather than a sort of intellectual patient whose school reports are more in the nature of a history of his disease than a record of his development.

The building will be of a kind which allows free and independent movement. Access to such things as books, equipment and other resource materials will be maximised. The student will be able to pursue his own interests under the guidance of the teacher. The class lesson will therefore be something of an occasion; certainly not the rule. Students will work as individuals or in small groups. There is plainly no need now for the closed box of the classroom nor for the one isolated teacher, implacable before a coagulate of children. Instead, what is required are working areas which allow freedom of movement, places where there can be discussion, and small withdrawal areas where counselling and guidance can take place. The chief characteristic must be a general openness of situation in which students may come and go from bookshelf to desk to specialised work-bay and so forth, while teachers may move among them informally and without disturbance.

It is good that the design is informed by this concept of schooling but good only for the future. As yet there is no community complex. In 1968 it was thought that the construction would be all but complete by the time this book was being written but one set-back or another has delayed the commencement rather than prolonged the time of construction. In 1973 there is not even the old established building. It was burned down in 1968. Since it seemed that the community complex was then about to become a reality it made no financial sense to erect a building which would require demolition almost immediately. The school was therefore housed in a series of 'portables'; temporary buildings made of light pre-fabricated sections which can be transported from one place to another. They have been the school's accommodation for three years so far. The work on the community centre is expected to begin within the next two years.

Initial interest in the plans for the community complex and the school accommodation within it was considerable. More importantly, the concern extended to what was necessary in the way of prior exploration if the school was to function as the building would allow it to do. The school as it was, set about an examination of its present curriculum and discussed freely with the Department of Education the sort of teacher needed to fill the roles required by the envisaged organisation. It also began to reformulate its existing organisation and curriculum within its temporary home. To make the exercise viable the 'portables' were modified in ways which allowed for a simulation of the 'open classroom' environment of the new building.

The core to the curriculum became a general studies programme which allowed for individual and group activity on the part of students and for team work on the part of teachers.[5] Special advertisements were issued in order to obtain staff familiar with such work. Here the interest in the projected centre was valuable. The advertisements drew an excellent response and a very talented staff was soon assembled.

One may sustain one's determination over a considerable span of time and lose nothing. It is much more difficult to survive with one's determination in full power when one experiences delay upon delay, particularly if delay goes hand in hand with increase of difficulty. Then one's sense of urgency diminishes and excitement ebbs away.

As the promise of the community centre receded into the future this is what happened to the staff of School A. The time to elapse before it would be possible to implement in full and under the right conditions what they were now creating in a makeshift way seemed always to be extended; it was always jam tomorrow but not today. Their impetus to examine and improve upon what they were doing was steadily vitiated and their pre-occupation was increasingly with things as they were. In the end it becomes all but inevitable that what is planned becomes more and more a function of the present condition and less a preparation for a future and different condition. It is therefore the more likely to be poorly adapted to the last. Yet, at the same time, whatever does not quite work out comes to be explained as a fault of circumstance and never of design; one's attention is diverted from the procedure to the context.

In short a school in temporary accommodation for four years or more ceases to think of itself as a school in transition and, perhaps even against its own better judgement, adjusts to its present environment as if it were its enduring condition. The promise of better things – of even the best of things – when continually unfulfilled yet never withdrawn, does not prevent this happening. It is doubtful that anyone can tolerate an indefinite period of time in one situation without adjustment to the immediate present.

One is left with the awareness that it should not be this way and this corrodes enthusiasm. Of the staff originally attracted to the school by the idea of the community centre, several key figures have left again. More staff have gained promotion or left the school for other reasons still. They have been replaced in the usual way. Apart from being unfamiliar with the destiny of the school many of the replacement staff have been new entrants to the profession.

Each year there is a degree of staff turnover; each year, therefore, a diminishing number of remaining staff have had to undertake the same procedure of induction and allow time for new colleagues to come to grips with the school's organisation. The school is running hard to stay where it is. It is difficult to build upon what has already been created let alone to turn to evaluation and improvement. Only the determination of a dynamic principal and a caucus of established teachers have prevented a collapse of morale and a deterioration of standards.

Simply placing an Educational Task Force team in School A immediately provides a benefit. Seven members of staff with considerable experience, together with previous knowledge of the school are secured for at least two years. But of course there is more than that. The school is placed in dynamic relationship with the La Trobe School of Education. There is a possibility of creative dialogue concerning what the school wishes to achieve. Taken at its lowest value this must represent a psychological gain and this is of considerable significance. Fantini and Young have commented that;

We are moving toward a recognition of the need for a more comprehensive diagnosis of the learning system as well as the problems of the learner himself.[6]

It would seem fair to say that the diagnosis could not be comprehensive unless it took into account the psychological effects of administrative decisions not only upon the learners but upon the ordinary teacher and the community of which the school should be an organic part.

School B

Much of what has been said of the area served by School A can also be said of the area in which School B is situated. There is a high migrant saturation in both instances and, in both, the immigrants are predominantly drawn from the Mediterranean socio-cultural area.

However no process of urban renewal is taking place. There are no immediate plans for anything in the way of public re-housing projects and certainly nothing in the way of plans for a community centre. The area immediately about School B is more industrial than that surrounding School A. The factories are comparatively large and long established. Residential accommodation tends to be interspersed among them in a maze of overshadowed side streets. To redevelop the area would require considerable re-zoning of land and the purchase of valuable sites.

Further to this, a number of main arterial roads interesect the area. Since the district is not far from the commercial centre of Melbourne these roads are lined with office buildings and large stores. There are no parks or large open spaces in the vicinity.

School B, like School A, began as a High School for Girls. Unlike School A it remains so. Its original building was of the same genre as that of School A. Unlike School A, no fire has destroyed it and there is no plan to rehouse the school. The site is very small. With the growth of population caused by the increase in the number of growing families brought into the area by the immigrant incursion, the same pressure upon school places was experienced as in the case of School A. The temporary accommodation provided to School B has had to take up parts of the already sparse recreational space.

The district to which School B belongs is no ghetto but it could easily become one. School B itself is no ghetto school but it has had to strive to avoid becoming one. Its task is made more difficult by the fact that there are competing secondary schools in the district, a curious situation perhaps but, nevertheless, the fact of the matter. There is no corresponding high school for boys nearby but, instead, there is a second and larger high school with a mixed intake. There is also a large technical school which takes both girls and boys. There is no selection procedure which formally assigns a child of the district to one of these schools as opposed to another: the single limiting factor is that School B is a single sex school.

Parents with female children about to leave the primary schools dotted about the area therefore have a choice of three schools to which their daughters may be sent. The primary schools themselves have a similar range of schools from which they may choose to advise the parent as to the child's post-primary education, for all the secondary schools draw upon substantially the same catchment area.

The sites of the other two high schools are more spacious than that of School B. They have therefore been able to expand to a greater extent. As a consequence they possess marginally better facilities and equipment. Somewhat larger staffs allow for the development of more diverse courses. The technical school, for example, develops trade courses which are directly related to the sort of work most readily available in the district and it does so in respect of both girls and boys. All of this enhances the reputation of the other two schools over that of School B. Not that the latter does not develop a range of courses for its girls or that these courses are less appropriate or well taught than in the other schools, but reputation is not bound to justice or reality. The marginal differences loom larger than life.

Many of the migrant parents bring with them a strict tradition of control over female children of adolescent age. Most families come from the pastoral areas in their country of origin. They are predominantly of peasant stock. To a marked extent these areas uphold a tradition of male supremacy and licence. The girl is fair game for the male yet utterly disgraced should she be snared and deflowered prior to marriage.

Anxiety over the adolescent daughter is therefore very much part of the family's life. A mixed secondary school at best appears to present a danger, particularly when the very restrictions upon the daughter in her home life dispose her to relish contact with the other sex within the approved situation of the school. Parents are therefore as keen to place their daughters in a single sex school as the daughers are keen to enter a co-educational establishment. If the girl does go to an all girl's school then the nearer that school is to a convent in its regime the better pleased are the parents. The fact that School B is by no means willing to play the part does not make its work the easier.

All of this taken together has had a certain and quite definite effect over the years. In the first instance the primary schools have tended to advise parents to send their children to one or other of the two larger schools unless special circumstances prevail. A sort of selection procedure of an entirely unofficial nature has grown up, by operation of which the brighter children tend to find their way to schools other than School B. Parents and primary schools have thus come to think of School B when considering children with problems of one kind or another, ranging from difficulties in learning to a predilection for sexual adventure. Little by little School B has stumbled unwillingly into a category of its own in distinction from the other two secondary schools.

The result does not require much description. School B's student population is drawn from a larger number of primary schools than the other two secondary schools draw upon and the intake tends to be of lower ability than the other schools. There is a higher incidence of behaviour problems. The parents tend to be less secure both economically and socially. There is more hardship in the homes and more of the homes are broken. The principal has become used to telephone calls from primary heads asking if she can make a special provision for this or that child who would not 'fit in' to the other schools.

As in the case of School A it is true to say that a school must adjust to a material extent to the circumstances which prevail upon it. As with School A a considerable change of circumstance overtook School B within a very short time span. Adjustment is then a painful affair. There was a period of low morale amongst the staff, a time of gloomily wondering 'what things are coming to'; a time of dark nostalgia. Many of the teachers continued obdurately to work as if nothing *had* changed or to work in the same, now quite inappropriate, ways on the grounds that this was to the only way to 'set things right again'. For example it was insisted upon that the school concert must still feature English folk songs and Elizabethan madrigals as a principal attraction.

Here we have an instance of resistance to change and of disorientation in the face of change. Inevitably the result is disappointment and disillusion, effects which produce in their turn, an atmosphere of persistent unease and tension. The curriculum and the manner of working of the school steadily parts company with the interests and understanding of the students. There is something tragic as well as ludicrous about the notion of introducing students to the culturally excellent by having them practice the music of another age, a country with which they have no ties, and a language with which they have little acquaintance. In the same way, to find oneself before a class with whom one is supposed to study an English classic and to discover that most of the children cannot read the title is a daunting experience. If one feels that what one is doing is right then it must surely be that it is difficult to avoid feeling that there is something 'wrong' with the children. When one finds further that the parents are ambivalent about their children becoming proficient in a language that is foreign to the home there is even greater discomfort in the work situation.

School B became a place haunted by insecurity, antagonism and mal-adjustment. Everyone was affected. Standards descended dramatically, as, of course, they must if what the standards measure is totally inappropriate to the nature of those who are supposed to attain them. Talk was always in terms of defect rather than difference. No one noticed the child who could sing the folk songs of her native land. There was no story in the language of the children's native land upon the battered shelves of the library.

Upon the retirement of the principal who had run the school for many years, her successor found herself faced with all of this. She also found the physical symptoms of the malaise. The recreation space was a dusty strip unfenced from the road. The original boundaries had long decayed. Dustbins provided the nearest thing to a climbing frame. Within the school the funishings and decorations had become drab or were non-existent. Books and other items of equipment were not so much arranged and displayed as piled or stacked. Staff accommodation was woefully inadequate. Lunch areas and social spaces such as the foyer were depressingly squalid in appearance. From beneath a crest that had been there for fifty years the school motto jeered down: 'Care for the Good'.

The new principal made an immediate and vigorous assault upon the situation. In the face of what might be called an educational ruin it is likely that nothing less could have brought any result and nothing less could have preserved her own sense of professional worth.

With considerable perceptiveness she made her first assault upon the symptom of the malaise; namely the state of the physical environment. Whilst it is undoubtedly true that what are now called disadvantaged schools do have ugly surroundings it is also true that, however inadequate the funds provided, the interior of the school says as much of the attitude within it as it does of the degree of support it receives from beyond it. To begin with it reflects the extent to which the degree of support has been accepted.

The new principal did not accept; she protested, complained, pleaded and downright bullied. She was aware that each time she gained a little money or some new item, she demonstrated that notice was to be taken of the school. The recreation space was properly walled, planted and landscaped. Attractive benches and a barbecue were provided and the dustbins were banished. Inside the school, walls were taken away, carpets laid and carefully selected curtains came to grace the ungainly windows. Curious spaces such as redundant but large cupboards and toilets were stripped to the bare brick, totally redecorated and furnished as small rooms to hold as few as four or five children and a teacher. Pictures appeared on the walls. The library was made into a library again and stocked with books of a kind which could be read by the child whose English proficiency was many years below her level of sophistication. It was also stocked with books in the language in which the child's level of understanding matched her experience and age.

With no promise of a community complex the new principal turned to modification of the existing school premises with the so far undeclared intention of suiting it to precisely the concept of schooling that was to inform the building which would eventually house School A. In this lay her perceptiveness. If a school staff must adjust to the circumstances wherein they find themselves, it makes supreme sense to change circumstances to secure adjustment towards the desirable rather than away from it. And to do it slowly. What was growing up about the staff was in fact the physical characteristics of the open classroom and the attendant provision of work areas, consultation rooms and specialist accommodation which would demand a new way of working. This was accomplished by ingenious adaptations of everything from a corridor to a cupboard.

The principal held regular staff meetings from the beginning. At first they were rather listless affairs, thought by many staff to be somewhat lacking in point. But gradually this changed as questions were literally forced from the staff by the continuing incidence of material modification just described. To these not always friendly enquiries the principal was able to reply in terms of her conception of what the school should be doing.

It became clear to the staff that a drastic overhaul of curriculum was intended which would lead to a way of working similar to that adopted by School A but shaped to meet School B's own special problems and characteristics. General Studies was to become a core. The problem of language deficiency was to be a dominant concern but the social and emotional difficulties of the children were also to be a prime care. Contact with the homes was to be assiduously cultivated.

The Department of Education grumbled at the principal's insistent demands. Staff left; staff resisted and complained; some staff understood. The principal called a halt to newspaper stories about what was wrong with the school, providing instead accounts of what the school sought to achieve, what it hoped to do in the future. Staff replacements began to include people who had asked to be placed at the school rather than those who could not avoid being sent to it.

Over a relatively short time the principal had accomplished the task of transforming one attitude to that of another across the spectrum of an entire school staff. That is not to say that all now spoke with one voice, that there were no arguments. Instead it is to say that talk was now no longer of what was wrong with the school, the children and the parents but of what it would be right to do given this school, its children and their parents. It is to move from the repetition of final and despairing conclusions to the asking of first questions. In short it is to create a climate for innovation.

School B was to receive the second Educational Task Force team. This being so, and since both School A and School B had more or less selected themselves at the time when the first Educational Task Force had yet to be created, an extensive period of planning and consultation could take place between the principal and staff of the school and the director of the project, together with colleagues who had decided to make an active contribution to this aspect of the work.

As is intimated above the principal was under no illusion that the problems of the school had been 'cured', and the staff were increasingly aware that there *were* problems requiring careful analysis and investigation. The school stood in a position of negative gain: it had checked and countered and ameliorated a sort of rot in the system and had, to a great extent, repaired the damage done. What was left to do was to effect improvement and change until positive advance was achieved, then to evaluate once more in order to understand how further to improve.

Even more than in the case of School A it is demonstrable from the history of School B that schools cannot attain an absolute point of rest. Schools in the circumstances of either of the ones concerned in the project are always in the state of becoming (to borrow a little from Existentialist terminology). Since there can be no state of rest it is all too easily brought about that there is a steady slide downwards as staff tire of the exacting task of improving upon improvement. Within any staff there are limits of resourcefulness and knowledge as well as of endurance. As the James Report recommends and as the Chicago Training and Placement Programme exemplifies, these limits can be transcended by support from beyond the school which is brought into the school. It is not a matter of assistance, sage advice or just an occasional helping hand. It is certainly not a question of mere encouragement. Participation is required, an addition of strength and a sharing of fortunes. A degree of positive commitment is essential. The nature of the Educational Task Force project is such that participation and commitment are built in components.

Of both schools

The fact that both the areas in which the two schools discussed are situated are ones which have absorbed a large number of immigrants from southern Europe over the last ten to twenty years, may create a misunderstanding.

To begin with there is no absence of native Australian children even though they may be in a minority. Secondly the native Australian child in these areas is no less likely to have educational problems then his foreign-born counterpart. These problems will include, indeed, will probably originate in, linquistic poverty resulting from the home's cultural aridity. In going to these schools the Educational Task Force teams were therefore grappling alongside the rest of the school staff with general problems of disadvantage and deprivation which are to be found in Liverpool or Chicago or Berlin. The problem is not that of immigrants alone.

It is important to realise that the children of the immigrant families of these areas of Melbourne are more or less indistinguishable from their native born fellows as they play in the streets and so forth. Their interests and their spoken language do not mark them off from the native born nor do they fail to associate with them. The differences lie in their home lives and in the networks of relationships into which they are absorbed as a consequence of their parents' desires and wishes. The children frequently live in two worlds and manage to do so with quite astonishing skill in a great many cases.

As has been said, the southern European immigrant found in the areas served by Schools A and B is generally possessed of a low economic potential and a corresponding level of education. Although there are cases where this is anything but true, it is also the usual thing that the cultural level of the family is of no higher a level than that of the native born Australian resident of the district. As a consequence the degree of literacy in the native language that the child possesses is frequently as impoverished as the native Australian child's proficiency in English. This does pose an additional difficulty but that does not mean that there is necessarily a difference in kind of problem. It has to be remembered that many of the immigrant children have spent a significant proportion of their lives in Australia and a growing number coming into secondary schools today were born in Australia. It is still the case that a language other than English is likely to be their first language but that is not to say that it is their preferred language or even the language with which they are most familiar once they attain school age.[7]

These points are made in order to dispel any impression that Schools A and B are in some way special cases and not comparable with the general run of inner-city schools or, for that matter, any schools wherein are found unexceptional children. They do have special problems but they are not of a nature which marks them off from other educational institutions.

4. *Team selection*

Special procedures

The schools which were to become part of the project were now identified. A working understanding and a growing acquaintance with the staffs had been secured. With the project formally approved it was time to turn to the formation of the first Educational Task Force.

As described in the first chapter, the Educational Task Force project consisted of building an advanced course in education around the work of a team in a school. Commitment to the task within the school was quite as much a part of the project as the study undertaken in respect of the academic units provided in the university. The latter were intended to serve the task.

The differences between this and the usual form of B.Ed. courses are considerable. There had therefore to be a different selection procedure for the B.Ed. Task Force from that for enrolment in the usual form of the degree course, admission to which normally requires the intending student simply to furnish documentation which demonstrates eligibility. Upon the merits of his qualifications in relation to that of other candidates and the number to be enrolled, selection is made. Later, the selected candidate may be required to meet one of the School of Education's Advisers of Study in order to structure a course to meet his needs and interests and to satisfy the requirements for the degree.

The individual candidate for the degree is committed to nothing beyond the payment of fees. He may choose to attend or not. He may discontinue the work and go his way. Even if there are some constraints upon him in all this in the shape of undertakings given to the Department of Education in exchange for financial assistance, he is still committed to no more than study.

Students accepted for the Educational Task Force were to be committed to work as teams in schools. They were also to work together as study groups in at least some of their academic work, notably the 'core course', a weekly seminar session based upon reading and study in the first instance and then becoming a research practicum, all based upon the team's function in the school.

Merely to scan the completed applications of the candidates for the Educational Task Force project would not have provided the sort of information that would afford an appropriate differentiation between people with comparable qualifications and experience. More would depend upon the sort of person chosen than upon his academic eligibility or his past record of teaching. No doubt the testimony of referees would be of considerable assistance but these again might not provide a clear enough picture. It appeared to us that selection in the case of the Educational Task Force candidates must be by interview.

The project sought to secure active co-operation between university, school and Education Department. Selection for the course involved selection of the staff of the school. It also involved secondment from one school to another – an administrative procedure. It did not seem appropriate to suggest that selection of the teams should rest entirely with the university merely because the project itself and the teaching to be given were the responsiblity of the university. Neither did it accord with the intentions of the project for the team to be provisionally selected by the School of Education and the selection merely to be endorsed by the school and the Department.

At the stage at which this was under consideration we were presented with one imponderable; namely whether or not there would be any great response to the advertisement for the course. In respect of School A, where the first team was to be placed, we had agreed upon a team of some six or seven members, a number based upon the lowest likely 'fall out' of existing staff from the school. (It transpired that the same number would suit in respect of School B.) If applications exceeded these numbers by very small margins there might well be some difficulty in forming teams of optimal efficiency and capability. We therefore placed the advertisement for the first Educational Task Force team as soon as possible after the project had received the several blessings necessary before it could be mounted.

Our worries about the response to the advertisement were proven groundless. One hundred and fifty enquiries were received and these were followed in due course by seventy-two firm applications. If anything we found ourselves with an embarrassment of riches.

We also gained a first indication that the project met a felt need, that it was not merely our own hypothesising that there was something awry for many people when they found themselves separately engaged in university studies in Education and practical classroom activities. In the application form we had included a section which invited the applicant to state the reasons for preferring the Educational Task Force over other alternatives. Many of the respondents wrote quite fully on this and there were many interesting comments on a variety of themes. However one note was pervasive throughout the entire range. Very few of the applicants did not echo it. The following extracts clearly identify this response.

I feel that the course outlined offers an opportunity to combine both theory and practice instead of studying both in isolation.

The choice of units appears to be more relevant to actual teaching conditions. Other forms of the degree demand a rather too 'academic' approach. The work to be done in this course offers a means of discovering more about the actual schools.[1]

With some seventy candidates to choose from it was decided to short list and interview two groups of twelve applicants. The interviewing panel was to consist of the principal of the school, the Director of Secondary Education for the Department, the project's director and a colleague for the university. Applicants were to be called to the school. They would be interviewed separately for some fifteen to twenty minutes. However they were to be asked to spend the morning in the school. Apart from the time spent in being interviewed the applicants would be free to move about the school, talking to staff and observing the school's organisation. This would also allow the staff of the school to meet the applicants.

So far as the selection of a first Educational Task Force was concerned the panel had very little to rely upon in the way of criteria. The various projects and experiments cited in the second chapter had all relied upon there being sufficient numbers of people willing to participate to allow selection according to possession of certain attributes such as psychological qualifications or expertise in particular subjects taught in the school. But even if there had been some set of criteria of a fuller nature than this it would have been dangerous to place total reliance upon it. The applicant who most closely corresponded to it may have also been the applicant least preferred by, say, the principal of the school. Plainly this would not make for the best of beginnings.

The interviewing panel was therefore to be its own judge of who should be selected, relying in its deliberations upon a nexus of considerations which were plainly relevant; e.g. sincerity of interest, understanding of the problems of the school, desirable competences etc. The project's director would also talk with candidates as they moved about the school.

No one was at all deluded that the adopted procedure would necessarily result in the best possible selection. On the other hand it did appear reasonable to suggest that it was a procedure which could be adopted in some measure in respect of staff selection for any school and this was considered to be important. As was observed in the second chapter, there was agreement with Getzels that far too little attention is paid to the placing of new staff in schools.[2] It would therefore have been unfortunate to have created a selection procedure that was either too complicated or too time consuming for general use.

But there was also a clear case for setting up some procedure by which this method of selection could be assessed. There was a need for some measure of the selected team's characteristics which could also be applied to all of the candidates. By observing the way in which the team worked once it was placed in its school and by comparing this with the measure of characteristics, there was a hope that a clearer frame of reference might be provided for future interviews.

To do this with any real effectiveness and validity it was obviously necessary to apply the adopted measures to other groups besides the applicants for the Educational Task Force project. Of the teachers who seek advanced courses in Education, there seems no reason to suppose that one form of course would meet all legitimate expectations, needs and goals. It would be of interest to see if those who did prefer the Educational Task Force form of course, possessed distinctive characteristics when compared with teachers who sought to join other courses.

A control group of some kind was needed. It was decided that this group should consist of a sample of teachers at large; that is to say a sample of teachers in schools in various parts of the city. Now among such a sample, unless specifically excluded, there is likely to be a number of teachers who have taken, are taking or intend taking B.Ed. courses, as well as teachers neither intending nor able to do so. We did not think that we should take steps to exclude any of these. It did not seem to us that to do so accorded with what should be meant by 'teachers at large' (Those in the sample who had already taken B.Ed. or were enrolled in a B.Ed. course could hardly be said not to have chosen the Educational Task Force form of course since this form of course had been non-existent at the time of their enrolment. On the other hand to rule out those who had, were, or intended to, take B.Ed. courses would be to assume that such people were so different from the general run of teachers that they must be considered as a separate type of teacher. This has not been our argument.)

It is true that the procedure lacked a certain refinement. However, it seemed unwise to complicate the project at its initial stage by introducing elaborate schemes which might not yield significantly illuminative results but would require a considerable amount of work which was not directly contributory to the work of the now selected team in the school nor yet to their academic advancement. Given that the first steps in this aspect of the evaluation of the project did indicate that there could be fruitful outcomes in such an investigation, then the crudities could be removed from the procedure in respect of later teams.

Particularly in the case of School B, but by no means exclusive to that one context, it was clear that parent attitude was a vital factor in the school's day to day working. Indeed there is a mass of evidence to suggest that this is the general case and much that argues that it should be a greater influence.[5] In the case of School B there was a period when the staff saw the parents as a counteractive force working against the intentions of the school. With the changes wrought by the new principal which were described in Chapter 3, that attitude has altered but this is not to say that the school does or could work entirely in accord with parents views and values. Rather, it means that school and home must interact, conduct a dialogue with a view to reaching a mutually valuable reconciliation of what may be initially hostile points of view. In order to do this it is plainly necessary for the school to be clear in its understanding of parental attitudes.

At the point in the project's development now being discussed it seemed premature and perhaps impossible to make any disciplined investigation of parental attitudes specific to the schools concerned. It did seem possible to make an investigation much on the lines of the survey of teachers at large. It was decided to take a general sample of private persons and to take a measure of attitudes to educational issues which was the same as that to be taken in respect of teachers. At a later stage it might then be possible to test parent opinion in respect of particular school populations and the particular areas served by those schools, the schools concerned being those in which Educational Task Force teams were at work.

Plainly the interest here is in such questions as whether teachers in general reflect the attitudes of the general public regarding how children should be educated, whether the innovative school is working towards or away from the views and attitudes of parents and whether those teachers attracted to the Educational Task Force project were more or less in accord with public attitudes to education than the general run of teachers.

The two preceding chapters have sought to show that what matters above all in the process of innovation are the attitudes that prevail for or against it. One would not expect the hard line conservative to be the sort of person who would willingly reformulate the procedures he had come to accept as best over a period of time and practice. Unless appropriate steps were taken he would be more likely, rather as with some of the original staff of School B, to continue to uphold the value of the established procedure. His concern would be for the upkeep or the regaining of standards in what had long been held to be of first importance. Furthermore, again much as the teachers just mentioned were known to have done, he would tend to insist that children adjust to what is taught rather than that teaching be adjusted to the reactions of the taught.

McLeish's very thorough study of students in initial training harks back to Eysenck's work on the identification and classification of attitudes.[4] This work is extended and modified by McLeish so as to have particular reference to teachers' attitudes to educational issues.[5] The teacher described above as 'hard line' (whether conservative or not), could be described as tough-minded in the parlance adopted by McLeish. When he exhibits the insistence upon adjustment to what is taught, rather than the adjustment of what is taught, he may be described as 'formalistic'.[6] McLeish's study indicates that a tough-minded approach to educational issues is frequently in intimate association with formalism. He developed special attitude inventories in questionnaire form to measure degrees of both these variables together with a number of others, among which was a measure of degree of radicalism in approach to educational issues. The resulting matrix of correlations furnished us with a great deal of guidance.

McLeish gives a table with the heading 'Security vs Change'. Immediately before it is found the following;

Arranging the variables in decreasing order of saturation co-efficients brings out the opposition between values associated with a concern for stability and absence of change and those which cluster around the desire for new experience and freedom from traditional restraints perceived as hampering necessary and valuable developments.[7]

By this table the variable of radicalism in education has a high saturation in respect of the desire for new experience etc; the variable of formalism has a high saturation in respect of the concern for stability and no change. The variable of tough-mindedness in education is also significantly connected with the latter although it is somewhat low in the order of saturation co-efficients. However, tough-mindedness in education has a further significance according to McLeish and this is of some importance when it comes to an assessment of selection of Educational Task Force teams.

McLeish comments:

. . . it is the committed, tough minded student, favouring considerable changes in the educational system who expects to gain satisfaction from working with children, from personal study and professional development.[8]

Now this appears to be a 'tailor made' prototype of the person for whom the Educational Task Force project is ideally suited. But it is important to notice that McLeish's comment tells of what the tough-minded (non-conservative) student *expects* will bring him satisfaction. It does not tell of what actually brings him satisfaction nor does it guarantee that this is what he can do more effectively than others.

For this and other reasons it therefore seemed inadvisable to use McLeish's inventories as an instrument of selection for the first Educational Task Force, even in a supplementary way. However, it did seem worth while to assess the degrees of formalism, tough-mindedness and radicalism possessed by those selected, together with all other applicants and the further groups already mentioned. It was decided to use only those of McLeish's instruments which referred specifically to educational issues and a schedule of these inventories was compiled and duplicated.[9] No attempt to distribute it to the groups mentioned was made until it was certain that it could have no bearing upon the selection of the first Educational Task Force.

When the inventories had been scored and once the first team had been at work for a period of time, it would be possible to make some assessment of the soundness of our selection of the team. If it did eventuate that the more tough-minded radical realised the achievements implied by his expectations as given by McLeish, then we, in our turn, could form expectations of future candidates according to what was revealed by examination of their attitude inventories before selection.

Of further and vital interest was a possibility revealed in McLeish's work, that the experience of participation in the project would itself have important results upon attitudes. McLeish found that educational experience gained in initial training for teaching does not materially affect what he terms the 'life philosophy' of students or their basic personality structure and that it would be 'unrealistic' to expect such a result.[10] On the other hand McLeish states that;

The educational values, physical, aesthetic, scholastic ... (which are almost by definition, not so deep seated as those appertaining to the accepted life philosophy of the students) are certainly influenced and change during, and as a result of, college experience.[11]

In terms of tough-mindedness and radicalism the changes are described as small (somewhat greater radicalism, somewhat less tough-mindedness). However, in both instances McLeish remarks that: '... quite small changes represent real differences'.[12] The finding regarding formalism tells a different story again.

The most marked changes are in relation to Formalism ... The changes here are of the order of 31.3 percentage points. It should be noted that the scores of mature students on entry are already low on the average as compared to the younger three year course (of initial training) students. It is an interesting question whether they are selected as 'mature students' ... *because* they have these attitudes to begin with or whether these attitudes are in fact those of a 'mature' individual. Our material unfortunately, can throw no light on the question.[13]

If experience of initial training, if the student-teacher, can be brought to be less tough-minded and formalistic and more radical in approach to educational issues, there seemed to be every chance that the Educational Task Force could achieve a similar result for the mature student, not only in terms of response to an attitude inventory but in terms of his actual teacher behaviour.

McLeish asks a conceptual rather than an empirical question in the passage just quoted, one which it seemed very possible to examine over the course of the project and to throw light upon where McLeish's material could not. The convervatism discussed in the first chapter may be seen to have connection with an individual's 'life philosophy'. As a necessary condition for the establishment of a reasonably stable style of life it must be distinguished from the rigidity of attitude that may occur once that degree of stability is secured. Given a certain necessary patterning of behaviour according to one's basic personality structure, life philosophy and, let it be said, circumstances and nature of occupation, where there is also a dogmatic resistance to modification within that context we may identify the reactionary rather than the conservative. Now a person quite unamenable to reason and unwilling to make independently rational assessments of his own procedures is not easily categorised as being of mature outlook. But prejudice is never entirely absent in any of us. It is therefore a matter of the extent to which appropriate experience leads to the alteration of view in the light of reason that is the mark of maturity. The Task Force project would seek to provide this appropriate experience.

By McLeish's finding it was reasonable to expect that those applying for the Educational Task Force would not be highly formalistic, being 'mature'. Secondly, the course description stressed innovation and intent to change; someone convinced of the value of the established order must surely be perverse to apply. However, McLeish points out that the measures are relative, not absolute. There might still be room for a reduction in formalistic or reactionary tendencies in the team and in those staff who were, by virtue of being in the school, participants in the project but not team members.

All in all there seemed to be ample justification for a concentration of attention upon the three variables selected from the large number dealt with in McLeish's thoroughgoing study. Measures in them would be of considerable assistance in our effort to test the validity of the many speculations given in the foregoing as well as to weigh the merit of our selection of the team for School A, which last endeavour must also be informed by observation of the team's actual behaviour in the school.

Team One

Inspection of the applications for the first Educational Task Force revealed that the project had attracted people from a cross section of educational occupations. There was a preponderance of practising teachers among the applicants, but, in addition, there were people engaged in teacher education, the Department's psychological service and the inspectorate. There were also applications from people in other states and a number from the private sector of schooling. From among all these was discovered a wealth of experience of the inner-city child and of migrants which was by no mean confined to experience in school.

The short-listed applicants were interviewed in two groups of twelve, each group occupying a morning at the school. Choice of those to be interviewed took time and consultation before the event and final decision upon the selection of the team rather more time afterwards. However, the entire amount of time taken did not seem to us to indicate that some such procedure could not be adopted in order to fit staff to a school, and this is an important consideration. To begin with the number of people involved was a function of a project much more complicated than straight selection of members of staff. Secondly it is doubtful that, in ordinary circumstances, a school would find itself with the task of shortlisting from such a large number of supremely eligible people. In the case of schools such as the ones concerned in the Educational Task Force project, as in the case of schools in Educational Priority Areas in England and the Chicago inner-city schools, that is to say in respect of schools requiring special qualities in the teacher as a consequence of less than favourable circumstances, the amount of time and administrative arrangement required to carry the procedure through seems amply justified and entirely practicable. The unwilling or the unaware teacher who is merely allocated to such schools is at best a risk and at worst a detriment. He or she is likely to leave again as soon as possible and, while on the staff, to do whatever is possible to minimise encounter with the very problems that the school may be seeking actively to tackle. In the course of this the teacher may become soured and disillusioned with the whole business of educating. None of this makes for efficiency whether we think in terms of administration of the system or in terms of the professional standing of individual teachers.

All of the interviewing panel had considerable experience of interviewing and all agreed that the interviewees displayed a marked degree of critical responsiveness in talking to the panel. They questioned almost as much as they were questioned and were ready to enter into a discussion upon issues which had plainly been reflected upon in relation to the course description they had received. Although neither aggressively defensive nor arrogant, they generally possessed the assurance needed to suspend their judgements about the project until they had satisfied themselves both of its viability and of their own impressions now that they had further acquaintance with the context and the nature of the work. (One candidate told the panel that he had reached a point where there were still some queries in his mind which would be best settled by talking with the staff while walking around the school. Could he therefore return at the end of the morning for a further discussion with the panel? He did this. The points he then raised were extremely valuable as a guide to the director.) It is agreed that what is involved here is the subjective judgement of the interviewers but the opinion of highly experienced people is not to be discarded on so slight a count. There was first evidence that the people attracted to the Educational Task Force were of a special calibre.

A team of seven was selected. Five of these were teachers from schools in various parts of the city. Two of them had responsibility for general studies in their present schools. Another was already a member of the staff of School A, although he had but recently come to the school. We saw his selection to be a particularly happy accident (for accident it was, since his selection rested entirely upon his merits and not upon his position as an existing member of the school staff). It immediately created a link with the staff. In addition it provided someone for the team who already possessed an insight into the school's general organisation. The two other teachers selected had subject competences needed in the school and had employed these in the teaching of children in areas with the same characteristics as that surrounding School A.

The other two members of the team selected were respectively a qualified psychologist who had been working for some years in the Psychology and Guidance Branch of the Department after experience as a teacher of mathematics, and a member of the inspectorate who, after hearing an address on the project given by the director and being present at the Department meeting which had sanctioned co-operation with the university to mount it, had announced his conviction that there should be further subscription to it in the shape of active participation in it and that he was not only willing to become one of the team but was also eager to be a member. (Perhaps it should be said that he, too, was considered entirely upon his personal merits and not in consideration of his position).

Of the team selected, five were men and two were women. Although the panel did not eliminate a superior candidate because of sex it did bear in mind that the school staff of the time was not balanced in a way which accorded with its co-educational intake. To have a team with more men than women was to make a move to correct this.

Three of the team selected were below the age of thirty years. None of these were less than twenty-five years old. Of the four over thirty years of age, two were also over the age of thirty-five, one of whom was more than forty years old. The panel had not considered age distribution in its selection but it had, nevertheless, selected a team which was interestingly in accord with a contention in the first chapter, namely that if the new entrant to the profession is perhaps not the most effective as an innovator in a school (even when he has very considerable potential as such), it is nevertheless probable that the younger established teacher is more likely to fill this role than the longer established. Subsequent observation of the work of the team might now be informative as to the extent to which age appeared to be a function of innovative effectiveness. Analysis of completed attitude inventories would also be interesting. Would the pattern across the team indicate a declining degree of radicalism and an increase of formalism and tough-mindedness according to the age of the team member? Report on these questions must await a further chapter.

The team selected was seen by the panel to lack one attribute which would have been desirable, namely the ability to speak the native language of the immigrant population of the area. Some applicants had presented themselves who had this ability. A few of them were felt to be unsuitable for the team despite this advantage, although each of these received very serious consideration before that decision was made. Unfortunately some suitable candidates failed to qualify for study-leave under Department regulations and their engagement in full-time teaching duties would have completely nullified their value as Task Force members even if they could have borne the load. The Department was not prepared to set a precedent by waiving the regulations at this initial stage in the development of the project. But, above all, the number of applicants who did have this linguistic attribute was very small. The language is not taught in schools as a general rule (unfortunate once more). Few immigrants from the area who come to Australia are qualified to become teachers. There is a very small pool upon which one may draw for teachers with this particular ability.

At this point it was not possible to say how damaging the lack in the team might prove to be. From the point of view of work within the school it was possible to argue that it would be of no serious disadvantage. There was one teacher with the language on the staff, selected at the time when the community centre had been thought to be more imminent than proved to be the case. She handled the children with a very small or non-existent grasp of

English. However, most of the children of School A did speak English fairly well and communication was perfectly possible. Their deficiencies lay in reading and writing English, a deficiency not exclusive to the immigrant child.

The real problem might well arise in connection with home – school liaison. The immigrant parent could be expected not to have a grasp of English in more cases than not. But even this is not the main problem. It will be remembered that the immigrant groups in areas such as that near School A seek to preserve a certain cultural identity in their new country of Australia. Contrary to some of the early assumptions made by Australian authorities, their immigration to Australia does not imply a willingness to 'assimilate' if, by that expression, is meant that they have no wish to preserve their own customs and language. The rather naïve view that this would be the case led to a notion that Australia could remain culturally homogenous although large numbers of people with no connections with the British cultural root came into the country. In fact their arrival has produced an increasing degree of cultural pluralism and this is, by now, generally accepted. Assimilation does indeed take place but not at the cost of abandoning cultural antecedents. To approach the immigrant in his home under conditions which demand that the immigrant employ a language other than his own is all too easily interpreted as a requirement rather than a misfortune and thus to inspire little confidence in the parent.

Apart from this one lack the team appeared to possess a range of strengths which could be expected to stand it in good stead. A third of a year now remained before it would actually begin work and some six to seven months before it would be necessary to think of the selection of the second Educational Task Force team. The time would be used to harness the strengths of the first team to the situation they would enter and then to learn from observation of its operation what considerations might be taken into account when the second team came to be chosen.

Team Two

The first Educational Task Force team was brought together on a mere three occasions before the beginning of the vacation ending the school year. Two of these meetings involved a number of School A staff and laid the foundations for the plans to introduce two of the innovations discussed in the second part of this book. However, much still remained to be done at the start of the year following which it would have been better to have had thought through in the preliminary meetings.

To allow the second team a longer period of preparation for its task in School B, the announcement of its intended formation was promulgated in July and the selection procedure was completed by mid-August. The number in the team was again seven.

Response to the advertisement on this second occasion was by no means as great as for the first team. Following some fifty initial enquiries, thirty firm applications were received, a number less than half that received for the first Educational Task Force. This was not altogether a surprise. The advertisement for Team Two was more explicit in its statement of eligibility, making clear that candidates in their first years of qualified practice would be considered only if they possessed attributes singularly valuable to the team which were not available among those candidates whose record of service in the Department of Education fully entitled them to study leave under the regulations. Although the regulations of the Department are available to young teachers entering service, not all consult them. Consequently some ten per cent of applicants for Team One had been ineligible on the grounds of insufficient service, among them a number who promised to be very suitable as team members excepting that they were relatively untried in the field. For the second team it was possible to persuade the Department to entertain special cases, should someone come forward with qualities outweighing that of experience. However, it is only the rare candidate who has confidence enough to present himself as such a case; in fact only two did so.

Many eligible and unsuccessful candidates for the first team were no doubt discouraged by their non-selection. Subsequent enquiry revealed that a number of others chose not to re-apply because they had become involved in their present schools. Others had joined the usual form of B.Ed. course and others still had moved from the area or left teaching altogether.

The fact that School B was specified as an all girls' school probably dissuaded some potential candidates. The arguments against segregation according to sex are cogent enough to make this understandable even though there was a reluctantly single sex school to be served whose needs could hardly be met by avoiding service in it.

By the time that the advertisement appeared there had been some public discussion of the work in School A.[14] It was work of a high standard and a novel character, but it was also demanding of talent, time and tenacity and discussed as such. The project was therefore revealed as a university course of an exceptionally demanding character. The understanding may well have daunted the over-modest as well as the poorly motivated.

Finally, the university itself had become a focus of attention at the time the advertisement appeared. Student unrest had attracted a good deal of adverse publicity. Some violence had occurred on campus and some arrests had been made. Falling upon this rather than upon the volume of agonised and responsible debate that it occasioned, a number of articles and cartoons in leading newspapers tended to suggest a state of internecine war within the university which threatened physical harm to all.[15] It is possible that this had some effect upon potential applicants for the second team.

In the end the important thing is that, of the thirty applicants, all but two were eligible for study leave and all of these were of a very high quality as candidates. Where the larger number of applicants for the first team could fairly easily be reduced to a considerably smaller number of conspicuously suitable candidates, the field of thirty for Team Two was narrowed only with difficulty. All fourteen of those eventually interviewed were of a quality commensurate with any of those selected for the first Educational Task Force.

Of the seven selected for the second team, four were men, indicating that the single sex character of School B had not discouraged some very good male candidates. Two of the men were in their late twenties and two were nearing forty. All three of the women were in their middle twenties. Team Two was thus somewhat younger than Team One when taken as a whole but this was by accident and not design, for nothing in the career of Team One to that date had indicated that age was a crucial factor.

The first team lacked anyone versed in the language of the migrant population from which many of School A's pupils were drawn. As was feared, this presented some difficulties for the team and increased its reliance upon interpreters when it set about work in the social environment of the school. Team Two contained a member whose first language was that of the migrant population in the area served by School B. He was a regular contributor to the Melbourne newspaper printed in the language of that group. Other members of the team also had varying degrees of familiarity with the language and were ready to improve their proficiency in it.

At the time of Team Two's selection a certain amount of very tentative data based on McLeish's work had been gathered by the director of the project, together with some reservations about its interpretive value. Some further discussion will be given of this in a later chapter and in a different context: for the moment it is sufficient to say that there appeared to be good reason why the results of the investigation based upon McLeish should not be given a governing role in the selection procedure. The director therefore restricted the information to himself and referred to it only when he had made his own choices upon other grounds. As a matter of chance it turned out that the match of team with staff in both schools was quite close in terms of scores for the three variables, although there were marked differences between school staff A and school staff B.[16] This supervised accident seemed to be to the good and best left alone.

Closeness of match of team with school staff had been much more deliberate in respect of other factors. Apart from the matter of language, a number of Team Two had worked for some time in inner-city schools. All were given ample time in the school to talk with staff and to assess their own reactions to the school's manner of working. One of the team had had experience abroad which included work with people of the ethnic origins of the predominating migrant group in the School B area. Another had, for some years, been part of a working party set up by a leading teachers' organisation to contact and work with migrant parents.

Team Two was composed exclusively of practising teachers whereas Team One had contained two members who had not been teaching at the time of selection, one being an inspector and the other serving in the Psychology and Guidance Branch. Whatever the merits of their selection, the Principal of School B persuaded the panel to the view that acceptance of Team Two by the School B staff would be prejudiced by including in it people who might be seen as strangers to teaching as well as to the school. The danger may be less in countries which customarily include upon school staffs people with roles other than that of class or subject teacher but the Australian situation is not of this kind. Partly for this reason one candidate was not selected for the team.

At the end of the selection procedure for Team Two there was again general agreement that a simplified process of the same sort should be the rule for attaching any staff to a school, particularly to schools with the difficulties and the aspirations of the two schools which now housed Educational Task Force teams.

5. *First steps*

Staff structure and team placement: two approaches

Not being supernumerary to the staff, each member of both teams had a dual or split role to play in the school to which he was to go. He was a constituent part of the Educational Task Force, a group intended to serve as an innovative and evaluative unit. However, beyond the let allowed by his study leave, each must carry a teaching load just as any other individual member of the staff, disposed according to his own specialisms and the needs of the school programme. As an Educational Task Force member he must be considered in relation to six others and that group as a whole considered in relation to the rest of the staff. As a member of staff he is to be thought of as a discrete unit of the total work force.

These two roles are not automatically compatible nor does one single formula for reconciling them suggest itself as best, at least in the first instance. The fact tempts one to the solution that the team must be supernumerary but, for reasons not without merit, this could not be agreed by the Department of Education.[1] That fact apart, there still remains a query as to the strength of the argument. An Educational Task Force attached to the school as an independent entity would be outside the staff in a sense. It would play no part in fulfilling the normal duties of staff except, as it were, by act of grace. The team's acceptability might well be put seriously at risk under such conditions since it could easily be seen as being in the school but out of teaching. The matter cannot be decided until some trial of super-numerary teams becomes possible.[2] Meanwhile the problem of fitting the two roles to be played by each member of an Educational Task Force had to be faced for both teams. It was resolved differently in each case.

School A: Team One. The staffing situation in School A has been described in chapter 3 and will be discussed still further in later chapters. It explains why, for Team One, the staff role was emphasised. As the school moved over the years from predicament to predicament along a stony road of make-shift provision, only a tiny minority of the staff in the school at any one time could confidently be counted on to be there two years hence. Most incoming staff would probably be inexperienced and almost certainly unversed in the practicalities of the school's open classroom and general studies approach. By contrast the seven members of the team came to the school with a more or less guaranteed life of two years within it; certainly with every expectancy of remaining for that time. They were experienced and gifted teachers who were to be further engaged in the study of new trends and ideas in education. Disposed through the staff in such anchor positions as co-ordinator of a subject or other teaching team it was clear that they could each exercise a guiding and stabilising influence and this would surely be in total accord with the rationale informing the Educational Task Force project. It would meet a pressing need.

The group would then have to take its own initiatives to achieve a working identity and form its strategies as a task force. Its initial undertakings would be formulated at the meetings between team and school staff to take place before work began in the school. Hopefully the group would augment these once they had gained experience of the school.

In sum, then, the two roles carried by each member would run in parallel, both being accorded equal importance and both serving the needs of the school. In large measure this was the mode of operation adopted for the team in School A and which had obtained for six months or so when serious discussion on the same question began between the principal of School B and the project director. The latter thus came to them armed with the advantage of having observed the way in which the organisation adopted in School A was working for Team One.

As will be described in some detail later in this book, Team One was by now beginning to achieve a number of things of value in the school. However, the question was whether its conditions of placement were helping the team as it developed this work and it became increasingly clear that this was not the case; what was being accomplished was more in spite of than because of the placement arrangements. Thus impeded, the team suffered a degree of strain which would have been much more serious in its effects had it not been able to fall back upon the support afforded by a project designed to buttress the teacher-student against just such adverse influences.

The extent to which the team members were required to act independently of each other in their teaching duties, forced progressively further apart the two roles which each member must fill. Each individual became involved in separate and time consuming aspects of the school's day to day work, with the consequence that the opportunity for and the apparent importance of work as an Educational Task Force was steadily diminishing until it was restricted to activities of a kind which could be carried on by one or two members rather than the entire team. This, in turn, had the effect of vitiating their sense of identity as a group. It was difficult to develop any initiatives beyond those which had been derived from the meetings held before the year began, a fact that would plainly have serious consequences the longer it went on. The team began with three main areas of investigation which had been settled upon at the meetings before placement. Initially these were approached as separate rather than related and the group sub-divided to deal with them, a sensible and effective procedure in itself yet one which did nothing to ease the problem now revealed.

The school's annual turn-over of staff being what it was, many of the staff were as new to the school as the team itself, indeed newer since the team did have some prior acquaintance with the school. Not having been present at the explanations of the project made to the staff of the previous year, they had but a hazy notion of what the Educational Task Force was, beyond that there was a special group among the staff. It is doubtful that they received any detailed explanation from the enduring staff or sought one. Everyone was embroiled in the move from one site to another which began on the first day of term, occasioned by the first stage of the urban renewal programme which was eventually to include the building of the new school. The portable buildings had to be moved some half a mile up the road and set down again on the edge of a public recreational space. A programme re-formulation to fit yet another change of circumstance had to be worked out. One gained the impression that working in the school was a matter of meetings to plan what was going to happen interspersed with feverish bursts of teaching activity demanding instant improvisation to deal with what was actually happening.

In such a situation no-one is confident and everyone is anxious. However much involved in the common dilemma they may be, special groups are regarded with some caution under these circumstances unless they show themselves to be particularly valuable. How could this be done at such an early stage and under such pressure, particularly when the placement conditions fractionalised the efforts of the group? Plainly it could not happen at all.

The concerted efforts of the entire staff under its indefatigable principal eventually brought order and some stability back to the school. Like everyone else the team could now begin to establish itself. But the inappropriate placement arrangements still hindered it and it was well into the term before the seven members attained a security of identity which lent them confidence enough as a group to seek to establish dialogue with the staff and to build upon the brief gained from the preliminary meetings with the principal. The first paper to the staff was presented at about this time.[5]

During the second term there was time and opportunity to discuss the matter of the team's disposition with the principal and to secure agreement that some modification of the arrangements was eminently desirable from all points of view. In the same term the Department of Education announced that it would allow the team members the equivalent of two days per week free of teaching duties in the second year of their work in the school, a very welcome recognition that what the team had now begun to achieve was of value and an indication of the readiness of the Director of Secondary Education to take a somewhat more flexible attitude than was sometimes supposed for him. Of itself the additional study leave obtained for the coming year constituted a difference of the kind required to solve the problem. Given that the team was timetabled to take a good proportion of the 'free time' it was granted as a definite period common to all its members, then there would be opportunity for joint work of one kind and another. The two roles would be very much less in conflict and both served the better.

School B: Team Two. There was almost immediate agreement with the principal of School B that the team was to be primarily considered as such. To negate a year's planning for and by the school, seriously prejudice the relevance of a specially constructed course and in any way to incapacitate seven specially selected people who came to the school to work as a group, seemed both absurd and dishonest. Of course, this was the plainer simply because there had been a year of planning, allowing for much thorough discussion of the school's aims and its problems. Reference to the Educational Task Force and how it might assist was often made in staff meetings, thus building the project into the thinking of the staff over a much longer period than had been possible in the case of School A. In addition the brief to which the team was to work was presented to the staff before it was seen by the team.

All of this increased the likelihood that the school would see the project as something in which it had a stake. Whether it would turn out that staff would feel this way remained to be seen and we were aware that some features of the placement arrangements could work against the possibility even though they aided the effectiveness of the team. In deciding that the team would work together in their teaching duties the special nature of the group would be that much more stressed and the prior involvement of the staff in planning for it might not offset the divisive effect this might produce. Every effort would have to be made to bring the staff into active participation and co-operation with the team from the time it came into the school. The team itself must come to the school understanding that a prerequisite to their success was their acceptance by the staff.

By great good fortune a newly arrived member of the School of Education showed much interest in the Educational Task Force project and chose to work with the project director in School B. As a first contribution he was willing to act somewhat in the capacity of what the Chicago project terms a liaison person, a role which Wayne J. Doyle describes as 'the single most important and difficult...in the programme'.[4] With considerable skill he proceeded to establish a firm and genuine relationship with the staff from which foundation he was able to take a position that stood intermediate between the team and the staff, being seen by both as someone possessed of good sense and ability as well as of goodwill. The achievement did much to smooth the way for the team. For his part the project's director fulfilled a similar function in respect of the principal and the team on the one hand and the university and the Department of Education on the other, where previously all aspects of liaison fell entirely upon him.

It was decided that Team Two should concentrate upon the first and second forms of the school, the pupils they would teach as a team in the school's general studies programme. As a task force the brief they were to be given consisted of the following.

(A) Evaluation of the appropriateness and the effectiveness of the General Studies programme: improvement and/or modification of the open classroom organisation.

(B) Assessment of the extent to which the school's accent upon compensatory education was informed by a valid conception or whether it induced a view of differences which inevitably turned them into defects.

(C) Investigation of parental aspirations in relation to those of the children and of ways of making home–school relations more significant to the work of the school.

All of these were issues which had pre-occupied the principal and staff in many of the regular curriculum conferences held in the school; occasions which it was now planned to associate with the core course for the Educational Task Force so that for at least a proportion of this central aspect of its academic work any staff who wished might also participate.

Prior consultations

It will be evident from what has already been said that the meetings held between Team One and the principal and staff of School A were devoted to different ends than those between Team Two and the principal and staff of School B. What had to be done in the former case had already been accomplished in large part by the time that Team Two had been formed, so that the latter began their orientation to School B at a stage more advanced than Team One had reached the year before. Team one had thus had more ground to cover and less time to cover it in than the second team would have. All this undoubtedly helped to exacerbate the difficulties later experienced as a consequence of the unfortunate placement procedure already discussed.

Team One. The series of consultations, although limited in number, provided an excellent introduction to the history and the problems of the school even if they could not hope to penetrate whatever social reserves there were between the parties at this time. However, the dialogues were rigorous and enjoyable. Later consideration of the matters discussed made it possible to formulate a brief for the team detailing the tasks it would tackle.

(A) Much work in the classroom was depressed in standard and limited in scope because of the pupils' lack of language proficiency. What might be done to minimise this bar to learning?

(B) Migrant families placed much store upon the privately sponsored schools set up in the area to teach in the language of the country of origin. What could the school do to secure the same parental support for the school in which the children of these parents spent their normal school hours? (The ethnically based schools operated in the early evenings and on Saturdays during state school terms, then more extensively over the holidays.)

(C) Among a significant minority of the student population (more native Australian than migrant), low expectations of and regard for schooling resulted in under-achievement and hostility even though the school sought to provide a free and friendly social atmosphere and a programme relevant to student interests. What more could be done to remedy this obstinate disaffection?

While this brief was being put together various of the university staff found one part or another of it to be sufficiently challenging and in accord with their own research interests to wish to associate themselves with the work to be done. The project thus spawned a team from the university which would also be concerned with the work in the school.

The problems identified suggested the academic units of study that the team should follow at the university over and above the core course which would be followed in weekly seminars at the school. It also suggested what of this range should be taken by the group as a whole and what offered as complementary options to be selected according to the way in which the team eventually came to divide its labours over the problems.[5]

There followed some sessions devoted to inducting the team into the organisation of the school and the allocation of teaching duties. The year was then far advanced and everyone became heavily involved in the many activities that a year's end brings. A number of the team found time to re-visit School A before the end of term and so too did those of the project director's colleagues who were to work with the team in the school. The director himself was also often in the school to follow up points raised in discussion and to shape a core course that was relevant.

Team Two. With their brief already formed for them the first meetings with this group took place at the university, involving only the team, the project director and Mr Bill Hempel, the colleague now working with him. The concern was to examine the brief and to select from the range of B.Ed. course offerings those academic units most appropriate for the team to take. After this, attention was turned to the content for the core course. Further meetings still were devoted to the construction of a reading programme to serve the group as a common base which could be embarked upon immediately. Finally, the meetings provided an opportunity for some tutorial work on the school as a social system, designed to alert the team to the problem of securing its acceptance within the school. Not many of the team had thought this through with any thoroughness. All of them came to understand that to think of themselves as a special group rather than as a group with a special function would be an error.

Having accomplished this much it was now time to arrange meetings with the principal and then with various sections of the staff, particularly those concerned with the general studies programme and with the first and second forms of the school. It was obvious that these meetings were better held in the school than at the university.

Towards the end of the final term of the year the team attended a day-long curriculum conference of the staff in which the place of the Educational Task Force was an important item for explanation and discussion. Prior to this the staff had had presented to them the list of topics for the core course and had commented upon them. It was now possible to produce an amended and final form which read substantially as follows.

We see the core of the E.T.F. course to be essentially based upon the reality of this school. We not only welcome but need to foster a dialogue which will include everyone in the school.

From our discussions we have identified eight areas of study which are specially relevant: each will be explored as thoroughly as time permits and until issues more cogent to the work of this school are suggested and agreed upon.

These are the areas.

(1) *How shall we see this student population; in terms of cultural deficit or of cultural difference?*

64

(2) *What strengths have we failed to notice and encourage in the students?*

(3) *Have General Studies a viable theory to back them?*

(4) *Principles of curriculum integration.*

(5) *Content and content presentation.*
  (a) The need for structure and the kind of structure needed.
  (b) Teacher input: child initiation.
  (c) What makes for a good assignment?

(6) *Learning and learning resources.*
  (a) To what extent is the local environment used and useful?
  (b) Can home-school interaction provide a learning context?
  (c) Is there any place for pre-employment experience?

(7) *Why do these children learn?   When do they choose to do so?*
  What do they learn?
  The E.T.F. will hope to provide some data from case studies using the following variables:

School	Home
Performance in school subjects	Parent attitudes to education/school
School behaviour and involvement	Parent attitudes to children and vice-versa
Preferred learning style	Parent competence
Reactions to teaching style	

(8) *Learning and social interaction.*

The preamble to the document was intended to make plain that the expression 'school based' which appears in the description of the course was to be taken to mean that staff participation was of fundamental importance. This had been said of course but now it appeared in a staff document to which there would probably be reference back at future meetings of staff.

The two briefs compared

With the exception that School B included examination of its open classroom approach and general studies programme, the content of both briefs featured much the same content. However the approach informing each brief was significantly different. That for Team One consisted of a series of innovative tasks drawn from a number of stated evaluations; that for Team Two consisted of a number of evaluative tasks, the accomplishment of which would enable the staff as a whole to make changes in its procedures, perhaps after the Educational Task Force had made some first trials.

Of the two briefs, that for Team Two was the more demanding since it not only invited constructive criticism of present practice in the school but also confronted the group with theoretical problems which were pre-occupying many educationists at just that time. For example the following two comments are drawn from a book published in that year. They are entirely in accord with the intent informing the brief.

> (a) ... the open school is inperfect and has many difficulties. Fortunately many educators ... have begun to acquire an interest in this form of education, so that, over a period of time, the open school's shortcomings may be remedied.
> (b) Compensatory education incorrectly assumes intellectual deficit ... and is therefore engaged in a futile attempt to remedy a deficiency that is more imaginary than real.[6]

So, too, is this comment from Fantini and Weinstein in a book published a little earlier.

Many of the processes established by the school (tend to) stamp out diversity, both cultural and individual, so that the urban school alienates pupils and keeps them disconnected from the school.[7]

It is greatly to the credit of School B's principal and staff that they should so clearly follow the spirit of Getzels' seminal paper[8] as to take into itself people from the university, together with the team, allowing them the opportunity to join in the exploration of issues which could yield adverse judgements upon some of the school's present ways of working.

This is not to depreciate the qualitatively different brief produced by School A for Team One, which called for action rather than evaluation. It also echoed concerns much to the fore in contemporary educational thinking, agreeing for example with Kohl's statement that,

... most defeated students, the ones most thoroughly oppressed in school (came) back year after year, looking fresh and open on the first day of school, ready to put their failure and despair and cynicism aside and begin again, if only it were made possible for them to do so.[9]

The pupils of School A were not oppressed in school and every effort was made to combat despair and cynicism. The school's aim was to make it possible always to begin again. But success was not total; the school looked to the team for new moves to improve upon what it was already achieving. By the time the second team took its place in School B much had been done to meet the demand and it is to this that we should now turn.

PART 2

Outcomes

Introductory Comments

Team, school and university

This section of the book is concerned in great part with the work of the first team in School A. Considerations of length apart there are good reasons for this concentration of attention. School A could not be thought of as being a specially favoured situation which would guard the Educational Task Force project against failure; in fact the only circumstance which could perhaps be said to favour the team was the comparatively progressive outlook which appeared to inform the work of School A. Even here something remains to be examined,[1] and, anyway, the physical constraints under which the school was actually conducting its open classroom and general studies approach were to no-one's advantage.

It is therefore fair to say that significant achievement by this team would serve to demonstrate the value of the Educational Task Force project. If difficulties which might well have defeated the isolated teacher-student were overcome and if the school and the university could work together through the team to solve or ameliorate problems, we would have learned much. Success would also provide evidence for or against the efficacy of constructing a university course for advanced students which had immediate consequences in their professional lives.

There is a further reason for restricting the section. The intention is not to furnish an extensive catalogue of procedural blueprints labelled 'innovations' nor to prescribe certain procedures as the only ones which will set the educational world aright. Plainly, the suggestion is that the procedures which were developed in Schools A and B do have value, but that is rather different from an assertion that they have some magical quality which is quite independent of circumstance. What matters are the insights informing the work and these are related to the circumstances of the particular school, circumstances which include the attitudes of staff and the aims and aspirations of the school. Much of what follows in the succeeding chapters is intended to indicate the nature of the innovative process. It is not intended to form a section of programmatic recipes to fit all occasions. What is described is not to be thought of as a number of terminal achievements, finished products no longer subject to process. The work considered here required much preparation, was necessarily slow in development and remains capable of considerable further development. One would not wish it otherwise, for these are the marks of richness in educational practice.

In many instances, members of a university's School of Education form ideas about what should happen in schools, design something called 'an experiment' and then go in search of a school wherein they may conduct this experiment over a limited period and in relative independence of the general life of the school. The school accommodates rather than incorporates the work from another place. Hence Getzels' criticism embodied in the distinction between university and school people and his talk of artificial meeting grounds[2]. The three colleagues who, together with the project director, worked with the team in School A most certainly had ideas as will become clear in the following chapters. But they did not use the school to test them neither did they bring a pre-packed schedule of operations to the team or that section of it with whom they worked. They worked in co-operation with the team members and the school staff to develop the idea in terms of the school, the team's brief and *its* ideas, then, in similar fashion, to translate all this into action.

As the team became thus engaged it began to develop independent interests and ideas. One of these had especial importance because it had to do with parental attitudes to educational issues and was thus relevant to one aspect of the team's brief that was otherwise not covered in any direct way. What became obvious to the team as they settled to their work both as members of the Educational Task Force and as members of staff, was that each and all of the enterprises upon which they were now becoming engaged was affected by this one factor of the school's relation with the home. (The same realisation is to be noticed as a governing one in the brief for Team Two constructed by School B. In discussing the one instance we are therefore providing a fairly clear indication of what was to happen in the second.)

Tasks of the initial brief

Tackling the problem of language deficiency. (A) As Dr Rado's account which follows makes plain, we should not fail to notice that deficiency in English does not entail that there is no proficiency in some other language. Secondly, it is at odds with common sense not to recognise that where there is a deficiency in one thing but proficiency in another which serves the same purpose, then the proficiency should be utilised while the deficiency is being remedied.

But there is much more to Dr Rado's idea of bilingual education than this.

The language learned within the family is intimately connected with one's cultural identity and there can be no more damaging a thing than to make a difference in cultural identity a defect. The insight which Dr Rado was able to bring to the team in this connection was invaluable.

The extent to which the team could develop the ideas about bilingual education was limited by the resources available. Happily the Department of Education realised the potentialities of the notion and gave this work the status of an independent project to be mounted in a number of schools of which, after School A, School B was the first, thus preserving the link with the Educational Task Force project.

(B) The School of Education of La Trobe University is composed of a number of centres for the study of particular areas of education. One of these was the Centre for the Study of Urban Education, under whose aegis the Educational Task Force project was launched. A second was the Centre for the Study of Educational Communication and Media which had but recently attracted to it as visiting professor, Professor Jerzy Toeplitz, formerly of the renowned film school at Lodz in Poland and the Institute of Art in Warsaw.

These centres were not intended to be water-tight compartments. Film is a medium of communication which is predominantly visual rather than verbal. It can be used with extreme effectiveness as a means of gathering, ordering and presenting data gained in the course of learning. Hence Mr Rod Nicholls came to associate himself with the team in connection with its task of ameliorating the effects of language deficiency.

The problem of the unmotivated pupil. We had to ask ourselves why it was that a flexible school programme, designed to encourage pupils to follow their own interests, should nevertheless not totally eradicate disaffection and hostility. As the first chapter sought to indicate, one root cause may be to do with the relevance of school as an institution; its stereotyped reputation. Where a youngster is convinced that schools can have no significance for him as a person there is very little chance that flexible programmes and so forth will make very much impact upon his attitude. One is reminded of the remark by a schoolboy quoted at the beginning of *Half Our Future*; 'It could be all marble, sir, but it would still be a bloody school.'[3] In that report much was made of such expressions as 'An Education that Makes Sense' and the notion of relevance, but the use to which such concepts are put is frequently unclear and prescriptive.[4] Nevertheless, as was discussed in chapter 1, a number of contemporary educationists argue passionately that the usual form of schooling is not and cannot be of personal relevance to the average pupil simply because school systems are linked to the needs and demands of the great 'people users' which gobble into employment youngsters who have been processed to accord with the development of technology rather than with the development of persons. Fantini and Weinstein, who are more reformist than 'revolutionary' in their ideas, are moved to describe the situation as follows: 'There are too many people to absorb as individuals; therefore a categorical depersonalized shorthand becomes re-inforced.'[5] Mr Szorenyi-Reischl's account examines more fully the implications of such a position and the efforts made in association with the Educational Task Force project to counteract it.

In connection with this work the adversities of circumstance suffered by School A did yield a benefit. The clearance which forced the school to begin its year by following its portable buildings up the road, left a number of small houses still standing in a waste of tumbled brickwork criss-crossed by roads. A chance enquiry by the project director revealed that they would not be demolished for some time. They were in perfectly good repair and still connected to main services. The school could obtain permission to make use of one free of rent as an annexe wherein could be housed the alternative school. (It turned out that this house was not needed for long. Another and more suitable building nearer to the new site of School A presented itself, the rent of which the Department of Education was prepared to meet. Yet, had that first house not been obtained we may not have sought the second or thought the undertaking a feasible one.)

Parental support. The chains of migration from southern Europe to Australia brought about a condition wherein ethnic groups not only tended to live in particular areas at least for the first years of their settlement, but to work in particular industries. As a consequence it became quite possible for a migrant to employ his native language both in his home and at his work. In many cases the need to speak English was minimal. It is not difficult to understand, therefore, that the schools set up outside the state system to teach in the native language the history, religious values and general culture of the ethnic group concerned, were seen to be important by the migrant parents and correspondingly supported. It is by no means the case that the students sent to these schools were universally as keen to go as their parents were to send them, nor yet that they shared the parents' desire and need to preserve a cultural identity. The fact only made the parents the more anxious that their children were taught to feel as they did.

Of course, support for these schools does not entail that the parents must have thought that the work done by School A was of no importance. The staff of School A was divided in its opinion as to the extent to which it enjoyed the backing of the parents.⁶ But, that apart, the team felt that there was much to be discovered concerning how far the parents *understood* what the school did. The open classroom, general studies and so forth; all this was very different from the essentially formal way of working that the parents were used to.

There was but one way to find out, namely by making contact with the parents in such a way as to encourage a free interchange of view. This involved a considerable amount of preparation for the team and required that they not only acquaint themselves with a growing literature about home–school relations, the background of the ethnic group which predominated in the area and the established contacts between School A and its parents, but that they also acquire certain skills and techniques associated with interviewing and counselling.

6. *Language in the curriculum*

BY MARTA RADO

The situation in an inner suburban school in Melbourne, such as the one in which the first team of the Educational Task Force worked, is a good example of the complexity of the problem facing curriculum planners in a modern industrial state. In order to understand the background of children attending such a school the team had to make itself acquainted with Australia's immigration history and present policy, the implications of cultural pluralism versus assimilation, theories of language acquisition and development with special reference to bilingualism. This is a vast subject area. We dealt only with those aspects relevant to bilingual education in Australia.

Bilingual education is a relatively new concept in Australia, not surprisingly, since until recently it could be assumed that most children attending school were native speakers of English. The relatively small numbers of non-native speakers of English made it possible to accept the *successful* school achiever as the typical representative of this group. It was generally believed that children of immigrants, irrespective of social class and country of origin learned English quickly and could easily made good any setback they suffered as a result of changing from one system to another. As the number of foreign children increased, the myth of such a magical quality of adaptation was gradually exploded. In School A today the idea would seem bizarre.

Language is central to the curriculum. Those who plan for curriculum change must give attention to the linguistic background of the children for whom programmes are prepared. They must be aware of the degree and nature of the difference that obtains between the children's language and the school language; in other words they must know the way in which children's oral and written competence is at variance with the norms of the official language they are expected to use as the language of instruction.

In the past teachers tended to treat such differences lightly, assuming that exposure to and insistence upon standard models would, given enough time, enable pupils actively to adopt those models. Speakers of a different language were treated with the same complacency. Maybe a somewhat more lengthy exposure would be necessary but it was thought that they would eventually acquire the desired competence in the standard language. All children were credited with the capacity of 'soaking up' the language if they so desired. Although today most teachers may not hold so simplistic a view, they still lack accurate knowledge about the structure and function of language and the specific linguistic background of their pupils.

Australian immigration: brief survey

Australia is a nation of immigrants of predominantly British origin. Until 1945, 90 per cent of immigrants came from Britain. Between 1788 and 1945 immigration to Australia was largely haphazard. British migrants were encouraged but others were accepted. Many of the latter were refugees from Europe. They came to Australia in the nineteenth and early twentieth centuries because of religious and political persecution in their own home-lands. Among them were Old Lutherans, Italian, Polish and Hungarian revolutionaries, Greek Activists, Finnish Utopian Socialists, Jews, Balkan Slavs and Germans. Even today Australian immigrants count among their number small groups of political dissenters from Portugal, Spain, Greece, South Africa and other countries.[1]

The so called 'White Australia Policy', enshrined in the Immigration Restriction Act of 1901, was an extreme expression of the desire to retain an identity fashioned on the model provided by the 'Mother Country', i.e. Britain. The image of Britain as a protector and provider survived long after she ceased to fulfil this function in reality. As late as 1945 Australian-born would-be travellers referred to their intended trip to England as 'going home'.

Consciousness of a British identity and the desire to retain it caused Australians to discourage the formation or continuation of separate and 'pure' ethnic communities. For example, when the Australians became aware that the Old Lutherans who settled in the Barossa Valley were seeking to retain their ethnic identity by setting up their own German schools, legislation was brought in prohibiting school instruction in a language other than English.

Australia has been called the 'lucky country'; lucky because it is a sunny place whose people enjoy a life that is relatively easy and harmonious due to a common language and shared cultural values. Perhaps the fear of Australia's immediate neighbours who are physically and culturally so markedly different, served to strengthen Australia's British identity. This identity is still very strong despite the influx of European migrants in the last quarter of this century, whose role in helping to fashion Australia's own self image cannot as yet be clearly seen. It was certainly not intended that they should change that image to any great extent.

When, after the Second World War, Australia embarked on a massive immigration programme it was first assumed that the newcomers would come from Britain. It was only when British migrants were no longer available that Australia started to look elsewhere. The displaced persons who came from Europe were a second choice. Their physical attributes and resemblance to a so called Nordic type played some part in their selection. Subsequently Australia tried to recruit migrants from countries that it considered ethnically close so that assimilation would not create problems. German and Dutch migrants were encouraged, then Austrians, Hungarians and people from other countries in Eastern Europe.

Only when these countries followed Britain in ceasing to be adequate sources of immigration did Australia begin actively seeking southern Europeans as migrants (Italians, Greeks, Yugoslavs, Maltese etc.). Of course migration from the British Isles still continued and has never dropped below thirty per cent of the total migrant intake. The intake itself has been a substantial one. It has been estimated that some fifty per cent of the post-war increase in Australia's population has been due to post-war immigration and the children of those migrants.[2]

Migrant education

Apart from setting up a machinery of transportation and hostel provision, Australia until about 1970 was content to reap the economic rewards of immigration while conveniently ignoring its social aspects. Since that time there has been a growing awareness that people who move from one country to another require specialised help to overcome problems and difficulties accompanying so drastic a change. A language difference compounds these difficulties.

It is curious to reflect upon how it is that the educational implications of Australia's change in immigration policy could be largely ignored until so late as 1970. Generally speaking European migrants in the 1950s and 1960s seemed quickly to become invisible. How could this come about? Were they in fact assimilated, having 'soaked up' the language of their new country? Did they subscribe to the view that they were under a moral obligation to become like ordinary Australians as soon as possible? The official view that assimilation was the common interest of 'old' and 'new' Australians alike was shared by the man in the street, including, no doubt, many teachers.

Since 1970 this assumption has been generally questioned, not least in educational circles. Ministerial pronouncements and the popular press reflect a shift in attitude from assimilation to integration. In the words of the Minister for Immigration in 1971:

The earlier desire to make stereotype Australians of the newcomers has been cast aside. The use of the word 'integration' instead of assimilation is not mere semantics – it is the outward sign of a fundamental change in attitude of the Australian government and people.[5]

Integration in this context means the recognition that the migrant, although still expected to fit into Australian society, has his own cultural contribution to make to that society. The team in School A were among the teachers who must consider how the school will receive such a contribution.

Whether an Australian today favours assimilation or integration, the retention or rejection of the White Australia Policy, there is unanimous agreement that all migrants should learn English as quickly as possible. It is also now realised that they need assistance in this. Why did this recognition come as late as 1970? Is this all that must be recognised? The questions are distinct one from another but the two become linked once one accepts the change from assimilation to integration.

Taking the first question first, the social backgrounds of the displaced persons and the north-west and east European intake may explain why these groups learnt English more easily than the southern Europeans who came after them and who comprise the dominant ethnic group sending children to schools such as School A today. Many of the displaced persons of the Second World War would certainly have learnt a second or even a third language during their period of displacement. Previous linguistic experience of this kind coupled with the desire to maintain social as distinct from occupational status (it was often difficult to have occupational qualifications recognised in Australia) would orient these migrants towards language learning. Even if many did not attain a comparable sophistication as in their native language they could follow their children's progress at school, would encourage their children to learn English and would allow them to speak English at home.

By contrast the southern European migrant with a rural background can be assumed to have had only primary education and no language learning experience outside that in his native language. Such a person coming to Australia must learn English in a 'natural' way; i.e. picking it up as he went along. In this he would rely heavily on job and other casual contacts. It is reasonable to assume that his language learning would depend partly on the nature and frequency of these contacts. In a situation of chain migration with the resulting clustering in inner suburbs and with the accompanying tendency of members of the same ethnic group to seek the same employment, contacts with English speakers would be greatly reduced. Moreover such groups in factories usually work under the direct control of bilingual foremen. Since they live near each other, the local shop owner would most probably also be a member of the same ethnic group. Women who do not go to work can reside in Australia for years and not learn more than a few words of English.

As was well known in School A, the children of this group, whether Australian or overseas born, have often not only language but general learning difficulties at school. In addition to greater difficulty in school adjustment the number of foreign born children or children who are first generation foreign descent have substantially increased in the last few years due to the different composition of the migrant intake. Whereas initially single males and generally young people without dependents or pre-school age children were encouraged to come to Australia, the more recent emphasis on family and chain migration has brought an ever increasing number of school-aged children to Australia. Some schools, School A among them, suddenly found that 'foreign' children outnumbered the Australian-British group. The government school survey conducted by the Curriculum and Research Branch of the Victorian Education Department in 1970 includes the following information.[4]

Main language spoken in the home	Completed years in Australia						Total
	0	1	2	3	4	5	
English	179	174	143	145	134	635	1410
Italian	713	759	669	645	672	2168	5626
Greek	1038	821	661	740	913	2658	6831
Yugoslav	1476	528	261	251	208	574	3298
Maltese	54	46	64	92	176	276	708
Arabic	126	93	36	27	17	37	336
Turkish	401	124	18	10	7	57	617
Spanish	145	55	32	19	24	66	341
Portugese	19	11	26	23	10	29	118
Dutch	113	119	79	63	54	130	558
German	173	124	118	113	89	246	863
French	188	158	121	58	21	46	592
Other European	270	196	94	139	132	350	1181

The general Australian public would have fewer more dramatic or frustrating encounters than the teachers of migrant children but given the growing proportion of non-native speakers of English in the country it is very likely that some such experiences are shared by all. The popular press in recent years has also helped to bring the plight of the non-English speaker out into the open. There seems to be general agreement on the importance of learning English, perhaps the most visible sign of cultural accommodation or separation in a substantially monolingual community. If one accepts Johnston's classification of assimilation into two types, i.e. external and subjective,[5] one can ask the question whether language acquisition belongs to the external rather than to the subjective category. We must notice that school children have no choice in the matter. Acquisition of English may well fall into Richardson's 'obligatory acculturation' category quoted by Price.[6] The rate and level of success in learning English may be closely related to opportunities rather than to interest and ability in this field.

Much more money, time and effort will have to be spent in future if the English teaching programme initiated and stimulated by the Commonwealth Government of Australia is to have its intended effect and is to reach all those children in need of help in schools such as School A, including those with a comparatively long residence in Australia. A foreign language home background, we have seen, may adversely affect the school progress of these children. The work of teachers must be informed by such work as the Government sponsored research of the Australian Council for Educational Research conducted by M. De Lemos.[7]

But is competence in the English language the whole answer? This brings us to the second of the two questions. Will competence in English achieve the widely held ideal of complete acculturation or invisibility so that the newcomer − or rather his children − will become indistinguishable from the rest of the Australian society? Is it indeed a valid ideal at all? Is it better if these children become monolingual English speakers with some contact with a prestigious foreign language (e.g. French) learnt at school as is the case generally in Australia? Is there any substance to the idea that bilingualism militates against harmony in a society? By maintaining a person's first language and adding a second, English, would we disrupt our culture? Does multi-lingualism lead to communal fragmentation and tension? These are questions of prime relevance for the teacher in a migrant saturated school.

Of course, historically, language has often been the symbol or symptom of friction in a community, the tool for expressions of ethnic loyalty. On the other hand, however, there is historical evidence that groups with a loyalty to the larger body politic ignore language differences.

Martin thinks that Australia already has a multi-cultural society.

Australia is not a plural society in the sense that our policy is based on ethnic segments, but in the more limited sense that ethnicity is a source of formal and informal groupings and of some cultural differentiation. Why has this pluralism developed and why does it persist? The responsibility – or what may be seen as the 'blame' – is sometimes laid at the door of the Australian community: Milton Gordon's 'prejudices of the majority'. It is certainly true that Australians have failed to build effective bridges between migrant and local structures and neglected the potential of migrant communities as genuine collaborators in the social process. We have also exerted pressures towards assimilation and against differentiation along ethnic lines. Such indifference and hostility help to explain the form ethnic group life has assumed, its weaknesses as well as its strengths.[8]

We may agree, then, with the words of the Commonwealth Minister for Immigration.

The English language should be a common link used in primary and secondary education . . . But measures must also be taken to preserve and strengthen the cultural heritage of newcomers so as to enrich and develop the sensitivity of the resulting new community.[9]

But what specific measures can be taken to so preserve and strengthen the newcomer's own cultural heritage? Do we haphazardly sample what is conspicuous and tangible, adopting on the surface some eating habits, manners of dress or sport, and do we offer the same things in return, leaving the basic acculturation processes completely to chance? What should teachers such as were members of the Educational Task Force team in School A understand by the Minister's edict?

Of course the problems we are dealing with are not exclusive to Australia although the Australian situation has some distinctive features. Country may therefore learn from country. Cultural pluralism is regarded in Canada as the very essence of Canadian identity. The Canadian Government has outlined a programme aimed at assisting 'members of all cultural groups to overcome cultural barriers'. It believes that 'histories, films and museum exhibits showing the great contributions of Canada's various cultural groups' will help to achieve this objective. A grants programme has been developed to assist such work. Efforts will be made to ensure that immigrants and their children acquire at least one of Canada's official languages. Moreover, research projects are envisaged which will provide greatly needed data concerning the precise relationship between language and cultural development.[10]

The Canadian Government has recognised that a language teaching programme on its own will not break down cultural barriers. Australians, on the other hand, have often been unaware that there were barriers. According to Martin the ignorance of ethnic differences among refugee migrants in the post-war years caused Australians to think of and treat all newcomers alike.[11] Australians today have become aware of the error. It remains for us to work out the detail of a cultural programme, at the level of national policy making and at the grass roots of the educative process of the nation, in schools such as School A. In just such places bilingual education and a multicultural approach should be put into operation to test its relevance in the Australian context. It may well help to overcome some of the teaching problems in migrant education which taxed the staff of School A and challenged the Educational Task Force team. About one quarter of our children at school have a foreign language background, in other words, are actual or potential bilinguals. In the inner city the proportion is often very much greater. Bilingual education must at least be given its chance. Consequently it was supremely profitable to examine with this team the concept of bilingual education and to take steps towards putting it into practice in an Australian context.

The concept of bilingual education

Gaarder has defined bilingual education to mean using 'concurrently, two languages as mediums of instruction in any portion of the curriculum except the languages themselves'.[12] Programmes developed in the United States since the passing of its Bilingual Education Act (Title VII, E S E A) vary widely. They generally aim at teaching skills and presenting materials in both languages. Learning takes place in the native language first, e.g. in the morning, and is then repeated in the second language in the afternoon. Some schools prefer alternate days rather than the morning/afternoon division.

The main participants in the programme are children whose native language is not the dominant language, i.e. the school language. In the United States these would be mainly American Indian and Spanish speaking children, but there are others whose first language is not English. These children belong to stable ethnic minorities who are American born. They are not new arrivals like many Australian migrants. Mono-lingual native English speakers are also encouraged to attend bilingual schools. The aim is not simply to upgrade the non-English speaker's school achievement, but also to improve race relations.

The change in policy from concentrating on teaching English to teaching in the mother tongue *and* English is based on the realisation backed by observation and research that learning in a weaker second language is a disadvantage. Language is so central to learning that lack of competence in the language of instruction can become a major factor affecting progress in all areas of study. The research data comparing the achievements of monolingual and bilingual school children in the U.S.A., Wales, and Australia show that bilinguals underachieve in all subjects not only in verbal subjects. There is one notable exception. W. Lambert and his group at

McGill University, Montreal, found that English-speaking children schooled in French did as well if not better than their peers schooled in English.

The conflicting data throw an interesting light not only on bilingualism but also on language and learning and the role of the school in promoting these. Generally a child does not receive tuition in the native language until he enters school. In English speaking countries this usually happens at the age of five, when the child has unconsciously absorbed the general rules of his language which will enable him to understand and generate an infinite number of novel sentences. Of course, his language will continue to develop syntactically until about the age of fifteen and, semantically, development may continue almost indefinitely. In other words he will absorb many more grammatical sub-rules. At the same time his vocabulary will expand.

The school can play a significant role in this development. It has the dual task of making the child literate and of supplementing the everyday concepts he learns at home and during other informal contacts he may have outside school, e.g. the mass media. The school builds on the child's existing grammatical competence in the native language. In countries where the native language is highly inflected, mastery of the grammatical system occurs on the average 1–2 years later than is the case for speakers of English. In these countries compulsory schooling starts at 6–7 years rather than at 5 years. This is justified by the fact that competence in the language of instruction is a prerequisite for all school learning, not just for learning to read (where the beginner is given reading materials based on the assumption that he can handle the language orally).

What happens if the language of the school is not the language of the child? What happens when native speakers and non-native speakers of the school language attend as a mixed group? The school might make some arrangements for the non-native speakers, but it generally works on the assumption that it can build on the child's general knowledge, on its everyday concepts and that it can do so in the school language. This arrangement often works superficially. The learner seems able to follow directions and learn a great many content words, particularly those with visually demonstrable referential meaning, e.g. names of objects, verbs of actions that can be mimed, adjectives of colour, size etc. In fact all vocabulary learning is relatively easy: and although it levels off after the veritable word acquisition explosion between 2–5 years, it never stops. Any adult could list a number of words that have entered his vocabulary in the last ten years because of technological and social changes operative in the world today.

A person's vocabulary is a necessary component of his language competence but it is not sufficient for language competence. Language is more than a store of words. Undoubtedly words are convenient labels or tags, they help to identify concepts and to preserve them in memory. But words derive their meaning as much from context as from the meaning we attach to them when we encounter them as isolated vocabulary entries. Any jumbled sentence spoken aloud will prove the point. The difficulty the listener will experience in understanding such a sentence can be compared with the difficulty a school child experiences when he is learning a second language whose grammatical system he has not completely mastered.

Perhaps this seems an extreme view which contradicts the assumption that, in such a situation, the learner will indeed misunderstand some sentences but would still be able to follow the gist of the discourse; the handicap could be slight and need not be taken too seriously. But the misunderstanding of some sentences and the understanding of others but slowly, like reading below a certain rate can affect the understanding of a whole segment of discourse in speech or in writing. The reasons are not cognitive, but perceptual. They are based on the biological foundations of language. Because of physiological constraints when we listen or read we must process the input within a certain time or we simply lose the information. The process is so fast that if we attend to every clue contained in the spoken or written message we are left hopelessly behind and information processing breaks down. In other words we must select the features we will attend to as active participants, grouping the discrete elements into larger units, e.g. words into phrases. In order to do this we must be familiar with the grammatical rules of the language. This ability enables us to finish other people's sentences or supply the missing word in a printed text. Unconscious knowledge of the grammatical structure of the language is essential for efficient listening and reading. In a second language, as in the first, the acquisition of such knowledge takes time. Trying to accelerate the process can create stress. It may be preferable to allow a more leisurely development in the second language and to build in the meantime on the child's existing knowledge, i.e. his native language.

Application of the concept in the Australian context

In places where the ethnic minority is a fairly stable, homogenous, language group, it is relatively easy to train teachers in the minority language. Early attention to the problem in the primary school may make special provisions at the secondary level less urgent than was plainly the case in School A. In Australia, children with little or no knowledge of English enter the school system singly, with a variety of ethnic backgrounds, at any time during the year and at any level. Therefore teacher centred bilingual education cannot be employed in Australia.

We could not, therefore, look to overseas bilingual education programmes to serve as ready made models. Nevertheless their modified form could be applicable and could contribute to the education of the migrant children in such schools as School A. If the migrant child is literate in his native language, bilingual education is feasible with the help of bilingual teaching materials.

In the Australian context there is the added urgency of bridging the gap the child suffers through the interruption of schooling. At an optimistic estimate he must wait six to twelve months before he can participate on an equal footing with his Australian monolingual peers in all classroom situations. Concentration on learning English cannot compensate for the loss in general learning. If there is to be equality of schooling then this loss must be made good later, requiring additional effort from a child who is endeavouring to acquire a native like competence in a second language and whose educational background is different from those of his native-born Australian peers. To complicate the matter further, there is a great danger that he will suffer language loss in his native language before his English has fully developed. At worst he will find himself in a linguistic no-man's land; at best he will resort to language mixing. Both language loss and language mixing could be observed in School A once the team was able to recognise them.

Language mixing and language loss

The phenomenon of language mixing and that of native language loss among migrants of all age groups is documented in the sociolinguistic literature. In two major research reports, Clyne describes and explains the linguistic changes he observed among German speaking migrants in Australia.[13] As his subjects were drawn from a varied sample of immigrants, e.g. early settlers, recent arrivals, adults and children etc., his findings could be accepted as generally valid for other migrant groups in this country.

Clyne claims that language mixing can be explained by interference and forgetting. The speech of all bilinguals is subject to interference, but this is negligible if both languages are fully developed and employed. Forgetting or language loss is due to lack of reinforcement or contact. This is the case when the larger community, the mass media and the school system does not support the native language. Even the highly educated adults are subject to it if they are cut off from the larger language community. It can be assumed that the process of forgetting is faster and more pervasive in children whose language is not fully developed.

If one adopts the point of view that language mixing is aesthetically unpleasing and cognitively undesirable then steps should be taken to minimise its occurrence among migrant school children. Hybridised languages such as pidgins and the language of German migrants in Australia, Italian migrants in the Argentine and others, show that language mixing results in simplification on the grammatical and lexical levels. For instance, the more general forms are used in both languages, so that regular forms replace irregular ones, endings are deleted, etc. This seems to be the reverse of the process observed in first language development, where the general rules are learned first and the more detailed rules later. These are the rules that make the meaning of the message more explicit. A language that does not possess a sufficient number of sub-rules may serve its speakers less well. Perhaps there is a correlation between devices available in a language for the expression of finer shades of meaning and the usefulness of that language to its speakers.

Apparently language mixing on the vocabulary level also leads to impoverishment in meaning. If words were simply tags for concepts then it would not matter what tag was used so long as one had the concept and the means of expressing it. But words are not simply tags for concepts operating as independent units. They often have more than one meaning, the appropriate one being indicated by the context in which they are found. The associative fields they can enter vary from language to language. Words like 'room', 'place' and 'space' are easily translatable into French or German; however, their associative fields, the words with which they can combine in a sentence, are markedly different in one language as opposed to another. In language mixing the likelihood that words will be used in just one particular sense is great and can lead to impoverishment at the semantic level. The complex network of associative fields can be lost. Thus a mixed language is likely to be less expressive and less flexible. If this were so then the migrant adolescent dependent on such a language is using a less efficient tool to express his thoughts and feelings than that employed by his monolingual peers.

There are further aspects to this disadvantage. Normally the school assists the child to refine and enrich his native language because it is recognised that his language is not yet fully developed. The migrant child on the other hand is stopped in his first language development. Instead of refining his existing language the migrant is under pressure to acquire a second language. This takes time and by necessity the advantages we associate with language refinement are postponed. In the meantime he must make do with what are essentially inefficient linguistic tools.

Practical conclusions

Give the migrant adolescent the opportunity in school to learn bilingually from the time of his arrival. Impoverishment in his native language is thereby delayed. He will continue to possess an efficient tool; there will be greatly reduced temptation to mix languages. His English will develop faster because of ongoing learning in other areas supported by bilingual texts and the beneficial effect a well-developed first language has on second language learning. The experiments with English-speaking children schooled in French highlight the favourable influence a well maintained first language has on second language acquisition and schooling in a second language.

Migrant children can and should participate in most of the ongoing school activities. (Where there is a heavy saturation of migrants there is something *extremely* odd if this is not the case.) Essentially the migrant children are not very different from their peers and should not be isolated from them. They will learn as much from their English-speaking peers as from their teachers. Nevertheless they do need specialised help in some areas. The special English classes are a recognition of at least one such area but another is that of continued learning apart from the learning of English; learning, that is to say, using the first language.

There is a diversity of school subjects and diversity of language background possessed by students. A wholesale translation of learning materials would not be feasible. It was therefore decided to focus attention on the language of the new immigrants and to design social studies type units which would provide the learner with information on everyday living, government, geography, history etc. A wide variety of information could be presented with the help of bilingual texts supported by visual and taped materials, attached to which there would be autonomous, self explanatory assignments. This was entirely in keeping with the general form of the work done in School A through the general studies programme. By adopting such a procedure the migrant adolescent would be in contact with learning materials of an educational standard appropriate to his intellectual development, that were comprehensible to him but which also contained a challenge which would stimulate him and extend his experience. It would be possible for him to gain a sense of achievement as he worked through them for they could bring him knowledge which he could see to be of value.

Criteria for units of study

(1) Materials should contain information about Australia that was both useful and interesting to the learner.

(2) Stylistically the text must fit the adolescent's language level so that it is not judged to be too childish or so complex that it obscures the meaning of the passage.

(3) Presentation must be varied to stimulate and maintain interest. Variety can be introduced through illustrations and taped materials.

(4) Active student participation must be encouraged.

(5) Check on student progress must be maintained. The services of an interpreter for say one hour a week in the school would be invaluable.

(6) The units must contain optional sections which teachers could develop into class activities. For example, a film on Australian Youth Culture or problems of assimilation could be shown to a class as a whole and migrant students not fully competent in English given a written commentary in their native language.

Description of background study units

The topics were planned to include:

Life Styles and Sport
Who can help?
Food
Clothing
Homes
Family
Festivals and National Days

All these topics provide opportunities for comparison between the Australian situation and that in the migrant's country of origin. They furnish tangible evidence that those in charge of education care for minority groups. They can be interpreted as paying respect to the migrant student and his parents. The bilingual study unit should enable parents to follow their children's study in some areas at least. Moreover, parents themselves might well find the material to contain useful information while, at the same time, providing through their English versions samples of standard adult English covering areas which normally fall outside the range of everyday conversations.

It is hoped that development of these materials will demonstrate the feasibility of bilingual education. It is based on the recognition of the necessity to ensure learning and proficiency in at least one language. It may not be a final solution but it could be an important component of a migrant education programme contributing to the intellectual advancement and personal well-being of this group of learners. It may significantly lessen the problems experienced by teachers in schools like School A. Its further development in that school and now in other schools in the inner city, including School B, will be carefully evaluated over the next year or so.[14]

7. Film-making as part of the Educational Task Force

BY ROD NICHOLLS[1]

Screen education

In not much more than fifty years, the film has undergone three technical upheavals: sound in the 1920s, colour in the 1930s, and wide screen etc. in the 1950s. It has faced the entertainment challenge of radio, then television, and has developed consistently as an art form despite the interruptions of two world wars and that curious phenomenon of cultural flatulence which huffs and puffs to blow down any field of artistic endeavour to which its attentions may be turned.

However, in the last ten years a new and most dangerous challenge to the movie has appeared: the educator, determined to create historical figures of Chaplin, Renoir, Grant and Bundel before any of them are prepared to vacate the present. The sorrow rather than the amusement with which I greeted the remark of Pauline Kael: '... if you think the movies can't be killed, you underestimate the power of education"[2] defines my approach to the work in School A. Films are not ossifications to be analysed: they are personal, ephemeral experiences which need to be synthesised for comprehension. Even more is this true in relation to television, where programmes appear and disappear quickly and unnoticed between the advertisements. We look to make film and films available to the children: to eliminate the esoteric and substitute the understood.

The screen education course established as a joint venture between School A and the Education Task Force, has one basic object. It is to make the students *aware of the media*. The need here is for a word like VISUACY, which would correspond to LITERACY (awareness of, capability to deal with, words) or NUMERACY (awareness etc. with numbers). Although I find his verbiage profoundly irritating, McLuhan's writings about 'manipulation' are one-half of an observation which I would suggest as a justification (if any is needed) for the course. '... when faced with information overload, the only recourse is pattern recognition'.[3] Or there is Eliot.

89

. . . (previous) knowledge imposes a pattern,
and falsifies,
for the pattern is new in every moment,
and every moment is a new
and shocking
valuation
of all we have been.[4]

The students with whom we deal are both ultra-sophisticated and (at the same time) ultra-naïve about the techniques of film and TV. They have an uneasy propinquity with TV gleefully described by Richard E. Peck in *Films, TV & Tennis*:

. . . a (TV) viewer's reactions developed at home go with him to a cinema. He has been acclimated to technical devices and . . . traditions alien to the cinema . . . To this man's mind, slow dissolves from one scene to another no longer deepen mood so effectively; they pressage a commercial. A transition through a grey and black screen may lose his attention completely.[5]

They are utterly blasé about the media but wholly unaware of its effect upon them.

Film is an authoritarian medium. An ordinary member of a movie audience has waived his prerogative to control his own view of the world. The movie-makers will decide not only when he will look around to try to ascertain the source of that strange sound just heard, but *where* he will look, for how long he will look, and what he will see. There are two relations with this absolute control. One is megalomaniacal: Josef Goebbels or the endless repetition of advertising material, determined to influence the actions and/or beliefs of the observer. The other is expressed by Orson Welles, when he saw a movie studio for the first time. 'This,' he said, 'is the greatest train set a boy ever had.'[6]

Mechanics apart, Welles refers to the sheer fun of movies. Who has not enjoyed seeing, if not himself, someone he knows, on film? Perhaps the Apache were right to fear that the original daguerreotypes stole their souls. John Steinbeck observed:

I suppose there is no weapon which so slyly and surely attacks the souls of men as a moving-picture camera does. Men who are disgusted or hurt or just plain ignorant react to a Bell & Howell Eyemo as a frog does to a hot rock . . . it is a secret weapon which dissects people and brings out the curious childish ego that everyone has, and lays it spread out thick on the surface.[7]

Choppra has observed: 'Looking at our schools and the process of schooling, one must be struck by the almost total lack of zest and joy amongst children, in the business of education.'[8]

90

Learning by experience: 'People keep talking about the environment, and I've never seen one.'

In 1967, two Americans named Poignard and Mann took an old van and a movie projector and began what they were later to describe as the'curtain of illusion – the Odyssey of the Children's Caravan'. Their philosophy was simple:

Why not bring the theatre to the children in outlying areas, and use the film right in their home environment to enrich the vocabulary of IMAGES they so desperately need to form the concepts – otherwise meaningless – they will encounter in their reading?"[9]

They were espousing the findings of M. D. Vernon (1962), who stressed that: '... perceptual development depends essentially upon exposure to the patterned stimulation of suitable environment.'[10]

Academic unanimity on this point is impressive in theory and disastrous in practice. Wiseman[11] quotes Hunt (1961) who contends that by with-holding experience at certain critical periods of development, later perform-ance may be permanently lowered: '... every period along the line of developing must be critical for experience with certain types of circum-stances'. Holt quotes Hawkins (1965) and his idea of 'messing about', in which he claims that far greater time should be allowed in education for: '... free and unguided exploratory work (call it play if you like, I call it work). Children are given material and equipment – *things* – and are allowed to construct, test, probe, and experiment without superimposed questions or instruction'.[12]

The trouble, as always, lies with words. Teachers confuse the talking with the doing, or, at least, or at best, approach things the wrong way round – teaching a skill first, and then, says Holt, 'finding interesting and useful things to do with it'. Instead, what should be done is exactly opposite. 'The sensible way ... is to start with something worth doing, and then, moved by a strong desire to do it, get whatever skills are needed.'[13] Even when this is allowed in education, it is reserved for very young children – playing again – and is expected to drop out at later stages. Robert M. Gagné spelled out this absurdity.

The more varied these (stimulus situations) can be made, the more useful will the learned capability become. At lower educational levels, this variety may be achieved by deliberate use of various natural objects and events in the classroom, or on field trips. At higher levels, the function of providing contextual variety can be largely performed by verbal communication, of the sort that may take place in a 'discussion group' for example.'[14]

My own generation was already beginning to smell the rottenness of this second-rate offering, and today's students are telling 'higher level' teachers just what they can do with the meaningless experience of 'discussion groups'. The reason for the increasing spread of the movement is simple: television and film has brought to these learners vast areas of experience, and they want to employ it, not talk about it, or even go ON collecting it.

Hugh Cudlipp wrote this description in 1963:

The TV age child, simply by viewing, knows more about the world and its way than its grandfather could know in a lifetime ... The early shreds of learning and experience are no longer solely assimilated from the behaviour of one's father, who might be an oaf, or one's mother, who might be limited as well as harassed, from careless childlike questioning and from inadequate adult reply, from walking hand-in-hand to the end of the street to see the first car or the first bus ... these wonders and many more ... are nightly absorbed through the eyes of the very young from the TV set ... And the process is ceaseless.[15]

Not only these 'wonders' however. Bela Balasz showed with respect to film how our sensitivity had been recovered towards the human countenance.[16] The recovery was needed. 'The linear, eye-dropper flow of printed words', says McLuhan, 'had greatly weakened the plastic powers and iconic perception'.[17]

The theories of both Edward L. Thorndike and Edwin R. Guthrie, did they but know it, explain this kind of learning state. Both cover the scatter-gun effect of what John Grierson called 'transfer of belief' from one set of images to another, or from information derived from the screen to actuality.[18] Grierson at the time, was referring to the transfer from documentary film to fiction film. Once you've seen somebody get shot, Kean-like heroic deaths become ridiculous. (This reaction against stylisation in favour of the actual is another part of the forthcoming defeat of the word. As Abel Gance anticipated: 'The time of the image has come.'[19] Guthrie's learning 'law' is a duplicate of this transfer theory, and Thorndike, having based his case on trial and error, or as he called it later, selecting and connecting, added the rider of 'associative shifting'. After seeing or doing anything often enough, he says, the learner can fill in gaps for himself. Hilgard quotes him as follows: 'We may get any response of which a learner is capable associated with any situation to which he is sensitive.'[20]

The role of the teacher as a kind of Delphian oracle has passed to the other media of communication, which are probably more reliable than the teacher in any case. Now the teacher must become a guide and a help in the individual's learning life.

In their book, *Designing Education for Tomorrow's Cities*, Fantini and Young relate four categories of targets – educational activities which have reference to the general areas in which the student will lead his life.[21] These are, basically:

(1) Skill development
(2) Growth in social participation
(3) Development of personal talents and interests
(4) Explorations of self

From my biased view as a screen educator, I would suggest that film could be related to all four of these areas in a school such as School A, but the third would seem to be both the most generally important and the most relevant to the specific school in which we worked. At School A we could open up options in respect of the third 'target' which promised to serve a particularly valuable purpose.

Fantini and Young expand their third point thus:

Rather than a formal sequence of knowledge, students will learn content in relation to their interests and projects. In this area children will be concerned with such activities as play-writing, movie-making, learning to play a musical instrument, bridge building . . . developing stamp collections etc.[22]

All these activities do indeed have their value. I would select music and stamp-collecting as being of particular relevance on positive and negative grounds respectively. John Holt makes positive assertions for children learning to play a 'cello in his book *How Children Learn*.[23] He describes how relationships can be rapidly established between hands, the bow, the string, and so on, pointing out that these relationships have been discovered while the child has been constantly active. No doubt, as Holt admits, much that the child discovers is not useful although it is fun, but even the scientist is today set against the false economy of science teaching which drives for the 'correct result' at the expense of the activity of experiment.

To emphasise the process of work was part of the film work at School A. Here there is reason to remark on the negative grounds for the value of Fantini and Young's 'stamp collecting' activity as it applies to screen education. John C. Murray attacked film making in 'film appreciation' courses on the grounds that they in no way contributed to the student's capacity to discuss the film in question and the student's enjoyment was no more relevant to educational value than 'stamp collecting'.[24] I think Mr Holt might join me in murmuring 'quite so' – no more and no less relevant than an activity sprung from interest and permitting the exercise of talents.

How can film be employed?

Five ways occur immediately.

(1) In enhancing the student's self image and making available that image to educators. Many of the children live in deprived homes where there is likely to be either negative feedback for them to form an impression of themselves, or direct pressure against such a formation in terms of emphasis on conformity and obedience.

(2) Where the idea of community has been lost in a situation of arid movements to 'urban renewal', film could bring back that sense of 'habitation' which is the prime loss. We may achieve images relating creatively to 'urban claustrophobia'. Indeed the very nature of high-rise living offers unique visual possibilities that are likely to enhance the creation of an environmental image enabling the students to SEE their surroundings for the first time. Both this and the previous point are integral parts of the quest for 'What is an Australian?' a 3rd Form project in general studies. They offer the two counter-questions: 'Am I an Australian?' and 'Where is Australia?'

(3) Film-making makes possible the breaking of the tyranny of words in education. The teacher can be accepted if he communicates with a visual capacity not markedly superior to that of the pupils (relieving considerations of insubordination – see Point 5 below), and at least *tries* to rid himself of what John Holt calls 'the grip of an astonishing delusion. We think we can take a picture, a structure, a working model of something constructed in our minds out of long experience and familiarity, and by turning the model into a string of words, transplant it whole into the mind of somebody else'.[25] As a teacher uneasy with much conversation, and one who finds words often recalcitrant, I hoped to top the children's withdrawal from a talk ridden situation with my own and meet them coming back. It's a tricky process but some worthwhile results had already been achieved in a model course in screen education I had established with one High School near the university.

(4) In the matter of 'parent education', film can bring a new dimension to home–school relations. Schools should be centres for a good deal of parent education in that all parents have some connection with them for a number of years. A high proportion of School A's parents are 'New Australians' as the coy phrase has it, and they are undoubtedly affected by the same language pressures as discussed in my previous point above (3) and more fully again in other chapters of this book, especially chapters 5 and 8. The direct contact which can be made by films originated by their own children,

without the flimsy intermediacy of words can result in a good deal of new communication.

(5) Finally, but possibly most importantly, film is in its nature anti-authoritarian in its making even though, as I have said earlier, it can exercise a certain authoritarianism as a medium, particularly in respect of the uninformed cinema-goer. For the success of the means of communication advanced in my third point, there must be no question of rank between the teacher and the student. The malaise of the feeling that 'you can't beat the system' observed by Choppra[26] and detailed by Fantini and Young in terms of eternal bureaucratic forms 'increasing significantly ... if you are a member of a minority group',[27] can be cracked if the system is ignored. (In my view it is all it deserves in any case.) Movies make form-filling impossible and self-expression accessible to otherwise lackadaisical members of minority groups, and cut across that division into opposing groups of students who are respectively:

a. completely independent, even aggressive
b. completely dependent and unable to do anything for themselves.

Film needs both autocrats and extras, and the line between the two categories is, in my experience, often erratic over time: people simply change categories.

The form of the work

Robert M. Gagne[28] has written that the 'motivation to achieve means wanting to be able to do something'. Stan Doenau records that teachers do not have a monopoly of teaching and that where there is free communication in small groups the way is open for students to teach each other.[29] Richardson says of group methods that they yield significant gains in co-operative attitudes as well as in achievement when compared with the conventionally taught 'class'.[30] Ruth Beard comments on the plateaux of skill acquirement that are to be expected and upon the subsequent surge of rapid improvement.[31]

One activity pulls all these disparate influences together and turns them into positives; the activity of film-making. There is ample opportunity for the mastery of individual skills; e.g. camera – subdivide into focus, lightmeter operation etc. Everyone can master and be seen to have mastered something. Amongst all these skills rubbing shoulders, there is bound to be cross-fertilisation. People will teach other people what they are doing as much as a a matter of pride as of anything else. Working to make a film has always had marvellous effects on people's characters in my experience. The group does not become 'over-valued', to use Freud's term, because the film is more important; similarly, the leader (teacher, or preferably, the student-director) is not over-valued because everyone has an individual skill to contribute which is of equal importance. There is no need to counter hostility and anxiety by providing a 'common enemy' (usually another group) – the task is the enemy, and a formidable one, too. Information is fed to the group (the script, the theme), but the response is an individual one. Finally, film-making is a pattern of rhythmic action and inaction – corresponding to the recuperation periods which are suggested by Beard's 'plateaux'.

Individual artists are usually egomaniacs and often unpleasant people. That is why the art of the film is so suitable to education – it is a collective art, in which ambition has to be shared, and creativity has to subjugate the egocentric.

Making the films

Up to date, all practical film-work at School A has been set up in working groups of ten students. This approximates closely to my most desired pattern of work. In the first group, an uneasy calm preceded any kind of productive work. Two large Greek boys found it altogether too informal to call me 'Rod', and to do any other than take advantage of the opportunity to skedaddle to the pie-shop in our open shooting situation. They changed, however, and produced a script and most of the energy for the two complete movies produced by the group. One of these was a variation on a theme of the Three Stooges and has an irate husband bashing three men who happen to have asked his wife to tea. The romantic/sexual dynamic was completely undercut, not in film terms, for the movie's momentum carries it through awkward moments, but for the kids themselves. The 'wife' (Australian) and 'husband' (Greek) walked towards one another in the final scene of reconciliation and then comes a full screen CAPTION, 'The Kiss'. Murder in the name of fidelity is fine; holding hands in the same cause needs must be re-valued.

The second film is about Ned Kelly. It would be difficult to find anyone looking less like Mick Jagger than our star; solid, dark, perhaps Zorba-like. But the group knew its Ned, and arguments ran long and furious over the historical accuracy of it all. My own favourite moment of the movie is Ned robbing two charming ladies in the forest. It seemed cruel, and quite unlike Mick Jagger, to steal their only bag of flour.

Great arguments were occasioned by this incident (as, indeed, arguments developed over most points other than the armour worn by Ned), with

1. The smoke effect – among others

Photographs by Rod Nicholls and Draga Bedenikovic

2. In a Melbourne classroom, Dennis from Skopje makes up Miguel from Madrid

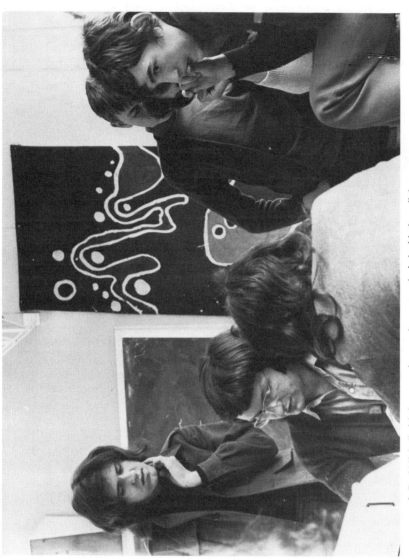

3. Rod Nicholls (sitting centre) preparing a story board with the collaborators

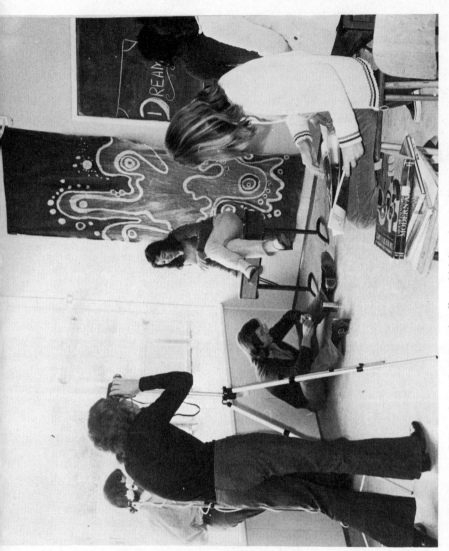

4 Preparing to shoot a smoke effect which introduces a dream sequence

historical accuracy eventually running a bad third to the more interesting principles of dramatic licence and practical necessity. For example, did the police kill Mrs Kelly? How many brothers Kelly were there? What crimes did Ned commit to set the police after him? How many men were killed in all?

The worst dispute came over Ned's death, which was done rather well by George Zorba mock-jumping over a good-looking white timber bridge in the park where the film was shot. 'No', said a minority of kids, 'he was hung.' One girl completely disassociated herself from the final part of the film over this inaccuracy. And THAT is being involved in history – isn't it?

The Educational Task Force member who worked most closely with me, took as a summary of our intent the phrase: 'An alternative to literary-based General Studies.' (See Page 71.) We initially devised three modes of this alternative.

(1) The production of conventional story films, giving students a chance to narrate in other than words. These films would involve several students and tend to be rather longer than those in the other two categories.

(2) Individual self-expression to which the literary equivalent might be poetry.

(3) Individual self-expression for students with difficulty in written and/or spoken English, who might be able to communicate concepts and feelings through film which are denied them by words.

In this last category I was to have an un-nerving experience early on. I spoke to a small group of students in a special English class and wrote out some basic film terms. There seemed to me to be absolutely no communication at all between us, but the class-teacher told me afterwards that I had managed what she called 'the most difficult task' in her situation, namely that of simplifying language without appearing condescending. This remark expressed in School A terms the difficulties analysed by Cruickshank and Leonard, who have noted the four most pressing problems for teachers in inner city schools as being:

(i) Lack of appropriate reading materials in the home.

(ii) Working with children with reading difficulties.

(iii) Dealing with children of limited vocabulary and speech pattern.

(iv) Inability of children to express in writing what they can say.[32]

School A is certainly not Australia's sole representative in sharing these problems. At School B, for example, it was discovered that only twenty of one hundred and twenty Form One students read to a level approaching efficiency for their age and sixty were not functional readers at all. In a report circulated to those concerned with the Task Force Project, Leslie Claydon, its director, wrote: 'The rest are "In-betweens" but nearer to the sixty than the twenty. There is little cultural support at home. Should one allow the supposition of a literary base to General Studies to stand?' Each of us had to find our own answers.

It is possible that when there is no real alternative to language, General Studies can be even more intimidating than older established and more specific areas of the curriculum. A combination of (i), (ii), and (iv) of the problems cited above from Cruickshank and Leonard can create in a child a feeling of impotence which is intensified by the very freedom allowed to him in General Studies. In this chicken and egg situation, more impotence is prescribed by the student's environment. The density of the central city, its mechanisation and depersonalisation are also evident in the urban school's large classes and the subsequent rigidity of procedure and recordkeeping. The area served by School A is an almost clinical example of Beers description of a community welded together by force of circumstance, not choice. 'What we once took to be the essence of community – common purpose, loyalty, integration, solidarity – are no longer by-products of adjacent habitation.'[33]

As a small attempt at restitution, School A's film-making has had two specific aims: firstly to give their environment back to the kids; and second to give them some power, in the sense that Stuart Hood implied when he commented that the more people manipulate the less people there are to be manipulated,[34] a point which McLuhan, with usual extra wordage, expands in 'The Mechanical Bride'.[35] School A's 'new Australians' are perfect examples of the 'prey' to which McLuhan refers.

At School A we tried to make one school's offering less 'puny' and to make observation, for a few fourteen year olds, more conscious. McLuhan wrote:

Ours is the first age in which many thousands of the best-trained minds have made it a full-time business to get inside the collective public mind – to manipulate, control and exploit it . . . since these programmes of commercial education are so much more expensive than the relatively puny offerings of schools . . . why not assist the public to observe consciously the drama which is intended to operate on it unconsciously?[36]

I am pleased to say that a very simple exercise can assist this. Take four photographs. Get two students to make up (different) stories which connect the four pictures. Analyse the differences: see how, say, a picture of a girl on a hill and a close up of a girl is used to represent the same girl by one story and a mother and her daughter in another. The girl on the hill is waiting for a lover: the girl on the hill is about to be shot. The children are *manipulating* the material to their own ends. For the first time they are returning serve in a game which has been run on them since they can remember.

Several of the student groups reacted unhappily to my suggestions that we try to use the school and the area immediately surrounding for most of our shooting. (It's convenient to do so, avoiding the necessity of organising cars etc. and it saves time.) They told me that there 'was nothing there', thus betraying their indifference to their surroundings, which is so absolute that they simply do not see them any more. The most criticised aspect of urban renewal, high-rise apartment blocks, are hated by most of the students, yet three of them became enthralled when it became clear during discussion that their new expertise in the use of a high-angle camera could find a wealth of application in attacking these buildings. It would be difficult to devise more visually fertile surroundings for film-makers than high-risers. The domestic minus becomes a filmic plus. When we filmed builders at work clearing the area to which School A had to move, close-ups picked out details of drainage ditches, a mechanical scoop, paving stones but climbing a tree achieved the top shot which one of the cameramen (yes, a high-riser) *insisted* was necessary to portray the lay-out of the site. If you are beleaguered in a concrete hutch high above life on the ground, one might as well realise the visual possibilities.

I found that the students could display a remarkable (to me) lack of sensitivity. The ecology bug has bitten deep at School A, and the pupils unanimously condemn pollution. We made a film about it – a seven minutes long record of terrible messes all within ten minutes walk of the school, and all known and listed by the students. They *said* that they cared about these things, but I suspect that basically we are talking about different things. Every one of the students defended 'bright', 'friendly' advertising signs (to me they were garish). They disliked Coke cans thrown on the ground in the nearby park – presently being carved into a waste land to become the termination of a new freeway – but realised no objection to the march of the electricity pylons across the grass. They professed dismay at the noise from an engineering factory, but played their cassette recording of the noises at full blast in the car on the way back to the school, defining, possibly, the difference between us. Their objectives were *ad hoc*, depending on the circumstances; my objections are in principle.

Perhaps one needs the *ad hoc* under certain conditions, as a sort of principle in itself providing flexibility of response to extraordinary circumstance. My own diary lends some support for this as well as demonstrating that it takes a special something to educate and be educated in the situation of schools like the one where all this went on. It reads as follows:

Arrival: the first person I spoke to was a drama teacher who wanted room 6 for the 3rd period. Would I transfer to the church Hall? I agreed – unhappily – as the kids told me that the Hall was freezing.
First period: cutting, thinking about music from records I'd brought along. Much enthusiasm. Argument over the suitability of the lyrics.
Another class comes in. The teacher asks if I'm supposed to be there. Strong affirmative. Teacher retreats wearily. Enter G.H. No church hall – P.E.! Room 17 is available. Room 17 has no power supply. Kids remain cheerful. One goes to ask for the use of the back room in the library. We can have the small room is the reply. Small? Who described a confession box as 'Slightly smaller than a grave and slightly larger than a coffin' This was a dwarf's coffin and eight people got into it, dragging editing equipment behind them.
Start work: no take up reel. Off goes Steve to look for it. Eventually returns, having found it in the Cottage, where it has been used by children from the 'Alternative'. This also explains why the projector box looks as though it has been trodden on. It had been trodden on.
Lunch time safari to the camera store to find replacements. But the films were made.

Conclusions

One of the most productive features of the work at School A was that it could short-circuit words, creatively and administratively. I am fortunate in that I teach a subject which fascinates me, and I think my enthusiasm helps a lot. I've tried always to persuade, not direct. On one occasion I wanted to cut out a lead-in to a shot which started on blank wall. Six frames could have conveyed the blankness, but the student director insisted on keeping five feet of the wall on screen (about 400 frames). So, after we had argued, it was left in: but I must have looked so disappointed (I *knew* it was a wrong cut) that the director suddenly relented, to the delight of the group, and agreed that my proposal was the better one.

Enthusiasm is a lusty plant, but it can bolt and die. It is not possible at short notice to produce people who are fascinated by basalt flows or who are made actively unhappy by a bad cross-cut in film. The students at School A are sufficiently astute to notice enthusiasm (or lack of it) and the Task Force has made capital of this. It takes time to get back a dividend of competence but there are signs of a yield now.

The Project Director has written: 'The university staff will develop their courses for the team, and any of the school staff wishing to participate, from the startpoint of the problems and difficulties of the school itself.' This is the essence of everything I have tried to say in this chapter. I do not necessarily believe in the superiority of film over any other alternative in the Task Force circumstance, but it has seemed to work at School A. Students are involved, and so are staff. Parents have come to film nights, watched, applauded, stayed to drink coffee and talk. The vice-principal has introduced film into his own classes, and the response has been good. We would do better if we had colour video, to give us an instant replay capability (the greatest moments of a film-teacher's life is being with students watching their own rushes). But that can wait.

What we have created already is a situation to which different kinds or types of children can respond, particularly two diametrically different types, examples of which abound in the areas served by Schools A and B. One school principal in another such area again has described these groups.

Much time is spent in middle-class schools trying to develop self reliance. With inner-city children some children are already very self-reliant even when they first come to school. However, another group is completely dependent and can do very little for themselves. Middle-class teachers are upset by the first group and annoyed by the second group. So far we have no technique for using one to help the other.[31]

I venture to suggest that film may be the technique for the task. The self-reliants become directors, scripters, entrepreneurs who wheel and deal to get the time and the stock they need: the dependents are bodies, extras, indisputably in the group, but not necessarily having to share the running of it. Autocrats and extras; as I've said before, the line between the two is variable over time.

School A's involvement with film is developing fast, growing well in not particularly fertile surroundings. Is there any other subject, or discipline, or – dammit – ACTIVITY, which could be so productive, so involving, in such a short time? One of the main features of my part of the work of the Educational Task Force bears a striking resemblance to an aspect of Mr Szorenyi-Reischl's; both film and the 'cottage alternative' are turning on the children to learning on *their own initiative*; i.e. learning rather than being taught. This is, to me, a major breakthrough.

8. *School: the cottage alternative*

BY N. SZORENYI–REISCHL

Introduction

If one considers that secondary schools as they have been and mostly remain, have considerable and fundamental problems in providing anything worthwhile for many children and a reasonable job-situation for teachers, alternatives have to be sought. The sort of alternative that will seem attractive will depend on what one considers the fundamental problems to be.

It is my experience that many school situations make life a misery for both pupils and teachers with consequent drastic effects on relationships between teachers and pupils and between children themselves, all of which leads to a distorted and harmful view of the world. This occurs supposedly, so that children will learn important things. Yet that must now seem a joke to anyone who understands something of the psychology of learning and the importance of internal motivation. The school situation of the kind I mention alienates children from learning, from each other and from a lot of teachers, and it alienates a lot of teachers from the children and from their jobs. In the end a few children will matriculate and join the happy life of the minor executive class. What about those for whom that destiny is unattainable?

At this point what one needs is a theory about which factors are responsible for some of these problems. One such which draws upon a whole range of experimentation in England and North America, attributes some of the problems to the size of schools and the consequent lack of flexibility which interferes with adequate relationships between teachers and pupils. It also points to the divorce of the school situation from 'real life' experience, a break which makes even the best presented subject material seem irrelevant.

Partly on this basis we started to think of a small, open-situation school with solid links into the outside world, i.e. jobs, institutions and adults, where teachers could act as personal and academic resources and develop close relationships with the children. My hopes were that such a situation would grow firstly some independence in children in being able to face the problems that their lives present them with and secondly the motivation to come to grips intelligently and creatively with these problems. I also hoped that the informal relationships developed in the small group envisaged would foster some self-confidence in being able to cope with relationships with other children and adults. And out of all this I hoped that a sense of helping each other to learn and to cope would develop. In short I hoped we would be able to break down some of the alienation of these children from adults and each other and from other aspects of their lives.

Initially these plans were free floating. It was envisaged that we would eventually set up a community school as a project and develop it to provide an educational centre and resource for children from a particular area. Then Leslie Claydon, who was initiating the Educational Task Force project at School A, was responsible for having a house, which was attached to the school, offered to us as a centre. Negotiations took place with the principal and staff of School A which eventually resulted in the State Department of Education agreeing to pay the rent for an annexe to the school. A member of the Task Force team was to be attached half-time to work in association with myself and another colleague together with a number of students in training under our care who would take part in the work as their school experience. The community school pilot scheme that we have developed in this association with the Educational Task Force project in School A is not intended as a recipe for all schools nor for all community schools. Rather, it is directed specifically at School A's situation and needs.

One presupposition underlying our work is that the required educational change must come with individual teachers and individual schools. Recipes for innovation handed down from the top seem largely doomed to failure because, unless one makes the programme one's own, the flexibility needed to adapt to one's own special conditions will never be there. People, classrooms and relationships are largely too complex for recipes and present schools too large for autonomous action. (Which is to say that we shared the conviction underlying the Educational Task Force project as a whole.)

In my opinion objective evaluations are unavailable for essentially this reason. Rather than attempt anything that would pretend to be an objective exercise it is my considered view that the need for something to indicate how the project worked with the children is most informatively met by presenting the personal evaluations of those working on the project. This in no way provides the objective evaluations that some consider to exist and questions on the validity of this evaluation must come down to the questioner providing his own evaluation. I have presented my own view here as clearly as I can.

Ideas

Eventually, if one thinks about what one is doing in education, one has to face up to how to make clear, both to oneself and to others, what one thinks is worthwhile for children. There are problems, for, although one might have an intuitive sympathy and grasp of talk about real persons, whole persons, developing potentials, or fulfilling needs, these terms are much more value laden than descriptive. Justifying one's values, and hence one's prescriptions, for the shaping of other people's lives, in an incontestable way, seems hopeless.

One way out might seem to be to let children make their decisions for themselves. But decision making does not occur in a vacuum; it is dependent upon people's awareness of alternatives and liberation from over-riding pressures. So, if one is to be involved in educational activity, one is committed to acting on one's own values and making some decisions about others on the basis of those values.

Further, if one is to work for the autonomy of the child one is committed to encouraging a practical understanding of why he acts as he does and what the alternatives are. In many cases one has to help him fight through the pressures on him, whether they are internal or external. In other words one must be involved closely with the social reality of the children and be with them in the real situations and decisions of their lives. It is not so much a matter of letting children make their decisions as equipping them to do so.

I have already declared my belief that standard schools have drastic effects on people's autonomy and hence their ability to understand and act in the world. I do not intend to defend that here but unless one does consider this to be the case then it would be best not to start by reading what follows but rather by reading the work of people such as those featured in a recent series of books on the ills of schooling.[1]

How one comes to be concerned for the autonomy of children is another matter. One does not have to approach it from the relativity of values nor necessarily from anarchist ideological commitments. Suffice it to say in the present context that unless one is committed to autonomy, then one would have to find a different rationale for one's educational activities and one's evaluation of School A's cottage or community school may well not be the same as mine.

The theoretical background underpinning the project has been expressed by Paul Goodman, Fromm, Denison and others and it is unnecessary to rehearse it again here.[2] Essentially it was considered important to provide a situation for children which would serve to break down some of their alienation from themselves, from others and from their environment. The school was to be a community school in the sense that it would provide an open situation for the children and adults involved, with opportunities and encouragement to integrate school experience with experience as members of the community, so that a greater practical understanding of the social environment might emerge hand in hand with some confidence and ability to cope with and change that environment where possible.[5] To do this successfully there had to be contact with parents, employers, public servants and people in general.

There was little information in Australia at the time on community school programmes at secondary level. It was thought that some information on this might emerge from such a pilot study as ours and also on particular problems in the Australian context. This project consciously differed from the other two community schools starting in Melbourne at the same time, in that we wanted to work in a small group, the others had enrolments of around one hundred. No less importantly, we wanted first hand information on how such situations work and their possibilities.

But other's experience overseas gave us considerable initial confidence and we felt that a pilot study of this sort would provide an excellent opportunity for teachers at School A to become more familiar with community school possibilities and thus bring changes in their own situation. There was also some chance that it would cause wider interest, with effects on other teachers, trainee teachers and parents. It will be evident, however, that the programme was essentially an exploratory one.

Procedures

I propose to look at the project firstly in terms of the indications it has given for working with children in this fashion, secondly in terms of the information it has seemed to provide for future action and thirdly in terms of its effects on School A and other teachers.

We tried to get a fair cross section of children from the co-operative to the difficult, from the intelligent to the less gifted. Even if one was most concerned with the 'difficult' and less gifted, there is something odd about putting all the difficulties together to make one big and isolated problem. We selected on the basis of school reports, from an initial list of volunteers and from teacher recommendations after parental agreement: but we failed to get the proportional intake of migrant children that we hoped for because of lack of migrant parent support.[4]

The house or cottage obtained had a number of fair sized rooms, a garden with a 'sleep out' or extension in it providing a further social space of some dimensions and some other outbuildings which were not suitable for use in quite this way but which could be employed in other and valuable ways as will be indicated presently. In the initial period we agreed that children would choose their own rooms in the house and decorate them. One front room was left as a meeting room. We hoped that this activity would consolidate the group, let them get to know each other, and us, and would start them into broadening activities, for example: having to come to agreement about colour schemes, having to start a bank account, having to work out quantities of paint and make fairly complicated purchases of equipment.

We then made attempts to introduce project work on ecology and population and another on pollution. Mathematical exercises were provided and English classes offered. The children were asked to nominate anything they were interested in and to write down what sorts of jobs they thought they were heading towards. There was considerable excursion work aimed again at achieving social ends and eventually a camp was arranged at a well known seaside spot. In the course of some excursions the children introduced the teachers to the area about School A. Visits were made to factories, other schools, both primary and secondary, universities, the swimming pool and so on.

Various of the children originated some of the projects. The property included a large shed which contained work benches and tool drawers. A group of boys set to work to tidy it up and to acquire the equipment necessary to carry out elementary servicing and repair work on cars. Some staff entrusted their vehicles to the group and were not sorry for having done so. A lot of planning and work went into setting up this garage.

One boy started on an electronic project. There was enthusiasm about having our own chickens and a fowl yard was built so that chickens could be purchased. Horse riding became very popular and the children organised their own regular excursions to the nearby riding school, making phone calls, collecting money and so on. They also organised their own party and their own parents' night. On a number of occasions the children organised their own morning and afternoon teas and cooked lunch. There was some initial enthusiasm in tie-dyeing and dress-making. The introduction of typewriters produced some enthusiasm for typing and led to regular typing classes over a period.

A film was scripted and produced by the children. Since then two films have been made on loneliness and old age in Melbourne in conjunction with a project on what it is like to live in the city.[5] A group food buying scheme may get off the ground and there are some indications of an increase in academic-type work which may or may not last. A project on working through the morning newspaper has started with subsequent lead-ins to job opportunities, available accommodation, car purchase, understanding of economic problems and political issues.

Somewhat abortive attempts at rule making were seen in connection with caring for the house. The children needed help here: youngsters who have been regulated do not necessarily understand rule making procedures or their value – often the opposite result is the outcome.

Our successes

Despite what I honestly consider to be the grave problems discussed later, I think that we have learnt a great deal – enough to be able to make a much better job of things from now on. I also consider that the children have benefited personally and very substantially. I suspect that they will have suffered academically very little: their motivation to stay at school and to work has increased and motivation is, after all, the key factor.

We might have tried to set up control groups and run tests to evaluate what we have done but, as I stated earlier, there are theoretical reasons to support my lack of faith in such procedures and my preference for the reflective judgements of people familiar with this and other situations. However, we do have some sentence completion forms which give an indication of the difference in the attitudes of the cottage children to school, teachers and other things compared with children in quite a large number of metropolitan schools. Insofar as one can interpret such data it seems rather favourable.

One of the better aspects of the situation is to be seen in the relationships between teachers and children. These are open and natural and make the job of working in the cottage particularly rewarding. Teachers can come to understand the children so much more and the openness makes one sensitive to mood changes and crisis points in the children's lives. This can allow for a lot more in the way of individual counselling, but most importantly it plays a significant part in how the child can relate to adults in general. In fact most children have very little access to open relationships with adults and hence take a long time to mature in this regard, with unfortunate effects on whole sections of their lives. Some children in the area of School A seem very aggressive and deceptive with adults and this seems to have strong connections with insecurity and immaturity in relationships.

The teachers who have worked in the cottage are generally agreed that as a result of teacher–pupil relations and as a result of spending a significant amount of time talking with adults on excursions, in shops, factories etc. some of the initial aggressiveness and deception has disappeared and has been replaced with greater openness and co-operativeness. There is a significant difference in this respect between some of our recent intake and the children who have been at the cottage since the beginning. This seems to me a major and long-term success due mostly to the flexibility and openness of the cottage situation itself.

Probably the most beneficial single activity has been the job experiences that the children have had. They have been intended to introduce the children to the realities that will face them in a few years and this has matured quite a number of them and given some of them motivation to stay at school. It has also broken down some of the romantic and unreal conceptions of what certain jobs involve.[6]

We had selected our group of children from the third and fourth forms of School A. Eventually, just when we thought it would never happen, the split between third and fourth formers disappeared and some sense of a community group developed. In disregard for such irrelevancies as age divisions the children have shown surprising concern for each others' problems and this has transferred to their dealings with people outside the group. What has been most encouraging are the particular developments and changes in individual children. We have observed them to have picked out and learnt important things from the wider experience that the cottage allows. This is best illustrated by reference to the case histories of four children.

Mary A fourth form girl, Mary came to us distrustful and immature. The only highlights of her life were the times she spent with her horse in the country. Her view of her future was that she would probably end up being a secretary somewhere but what she would really like would be a job with horses. Apart from horses she couldn't think of anything that she was interested in nor could she think of anything that she thought would be important for her to learn, except perhaps typing – a reluctant exception.

She confided one day, sitting on the kitchen steps, that she had difficulty in getting on with some people, especially 'wogs' (which term includes the southern European migrant groups). She felt a bit uncomfortable about feeling this way. Relationships at home were somewhat strained and she had an air of slightly sullen withdrawal in her approach to adults. She was friendly with two other children in the group but was very slow to make any contacts with the others.

When the offer of a trip to Adelaide came up Mary suddenly became involved and enthusiastic. She did a project on collecting maps and working out itineraries, gathering information on towns between Melbourne and Adelaide. Unfortunately her mother refused to allow her to go on the trip and that set her back for a while. However, the enthusiasm engendered had been sufficient to bring her out of herself and she started to lose her distrustful attitude.

We found her a secretarial job. She hated it and seemed pretty lost, yet this job experience made her a lot more confident in her approach to adults and she seemed to mature quite suddenly. She was a hesitant starter on a project which involved interviewing people about living conditions in the neighbourhood and about their residential aspirations, but it turned out that she was a much more competent interviewer than the others who were similarly engaged. In fact she was very good. This gave her confidence quite a boost.

Her success started us thinking that newspaper work might be interesting to her. So we arranged for her to spend a week with a local newspaper. The staff there got her to do some interviewing and writing up of reports. Mary was enthralled with the whole thing and the newspaper was very taken with her. She now wants to matriculate so that she can start in journalism. Her manner has changed entirely. She has confidence to make relations with other members of the group and has started to take the initiative in organising excursions. At the same time she seems content to settle to the hard slog towards matriculation next year.

Kevin This third form boy has not been one of our most unalloyed successes but something to the good for him has happened. He came to us as one of the most aggressive boys I have encountered. But he was small and the aggressiveness kept resulting in near self-destruction. Kevin lived in a dream world of being the hero and the leader, sexually aggressive and physically immature. His interests were toy soldiers, model planes and radios. I have never seen anyone so loath to engage in work of any kind, from helping to lift tables, to jobs, to school work. It was impossible to keep him from disrupting others engaged in anything serious because he wanted to be in the limelight. This aggressive and exhibitionist behaviour caused him to be rejected by the others and he spent long periods by himself.

He attached himself to members of staff but their lack of permanency in the end failed him. We discovered that there were no stable and enduring relationships at all in his life except one with an aunt who was very good with him. She died half way through the first year of the cottage. We made it possible to spend time with him after that. He settled a little – not to work of any kind, but he lost a good deal of the aggressiveness. He also began to be 'mothered' a little by some of the older girls and this helped him to re-establish himself a bit in the group. However he needs a person who is able to establish a solid and patient relationship with him over a long period.

John John was a very similar case to Kevin in many respects but was a more mature third former. We have been able to find some activities which he could do well – seemingly the first real experience of competence he has enjoyed. We managed to spend more time with him because his case was more immediately obvious at the very outset, but the time was still insufficient. We are in process of trying to arrange a painter's apprenticeship in the country for him and we have hopes he will pull through given half a chance.[7]

Marilyn Also a third former, Marilyn had incredible family problems. She is consistently sullen, she is bored, she is without interest in anything. Everything, even the excursions, are a drag. Other people are stupid.

It has taken till third term for all this to dissipate in some measure and for open relationships with others to begin to seem possible for her. Two things seem to have been responsible for the gain: having to mix with more mature people in the factory jobs and discovering they, too, have problems, and establishing a supportive relationship with one of the older fourth form boys, who genuinely takes care of her. We are very pleased with this personal development and although she will never have academic ambitions, she wants to continue at school a while longer to improve her job prospects.

Summary of progress

I consider we have succeeded in some part in breaking down some of the alientaion of the children. This has been evidenced by the way the children have enjoyed their year: there is a universal desire to be able to take part again next year, both on the part of the children and the teachers. The Educational Task Force member, for example, hopes to carry on in the cottage after the two year secondment to the project. The teachers certainly find the work more exhausting but we agree that this is more than amply made up by being engaged in a rewarding situation. The feeling of everything being against one and the sense of hopelessness, of being able to do nothing effective, is missing. The thought of returning to the irrelevance, strain and role playing of the normal classroom is anathema to all of us. (We do not here refer to the particular situation that is School A and its way of working but to the flavour attaching to schooling in general.)

The children tend to be reluctant to leave in the afternoon and they continue their close contacts with each other outside school time. A good percentage have had the initiative to organise periods of employment for themselves and have begun to look seriously at their own ideas about their working lives to come. However, we would have done better with at least one full-time staff member, a larger group of children, perhaps in the vicinity of fifty rather than twenty-five, and closer contacts with parents.

Our problems

(A) *Disciplinary*. The informal situation allows teachers to react more naturally, showing anger when they feel it, but not having to maintain discipline for its own sake any more than one would maintain it over one's own children.

Initially it was hard to get attention at general meetings but that has settled down a lot more now. However, there is still a major area of concern, viz. the children have not developed a strong sense of responsibility for the care of the house, nor even in some cases for their own or the corporate welfare.

This may be partly a maturational problem since the fourth formers show a much greater desire than those younger to care for things and be aware of the consequences of their behaviour. Nevertheless it is a matter of some concern to us and it will be important to try and pinpoint particular causes.

Some of the children have been involved in petty crime. This is a worry, but it is a general problem in inner-city Melbourne and there seem no indications that the cottage situation encourages it or prevents it, although I have considerable hopes that a properly run cottage situation *would* diminish it.

(B) *Academic*. Our academic problems have been more obvious, although maybe not as important. True, the cottage has been a pretty richly varied experience for the children; they have learnt an enormous amount about themselves, others and their physical environment − not nearly as much as we would have liked, but still a lot. Yet there also seems to have been so much inactivity. The children seem to have only initiated very trivial activities for themselves. We had hoped that there would be serious self-initiated activity. This is such an important thing, because they are not always going to have their hands held and unless they can develop some independent initiative they will just join the rest of the people who are receivers and never initiators; the do your job, watch television and do as you are told syndrome. They would rather be completely bored than do academic work and if you force them into it, they sit and do not listen. They will happily take part in excursions and novel activities if they are organised for them, provided they don't last too long. They will tell you that you ought to force them to work but obviously get nothing out of it if you do. They have lost nearly all the self-motivating drive they once had.

So things have failed to live up to one of our major hopes. The problem is why, and what can be done. Some faults and their remedies can be detailed as follows:

(i) One major reason for the inactivity mentioned above has been the disjointed staff disposition with its attendant episodicity of teacher-pupil contact. The task force member and myself were not wholly engaged in the cottage and the students in training worked firstly in two day shifts and then in three week blocks. This does not procure the continuity of contact with one person that is essential for many of the pupils I have discussed above. This has probably been our worst problem and I would not recommend such an arrangement. Diploma of Education students and others can be extremely useful as extra resources but there must be at least one full-time experienced person in the cottage.

(ii) Third and Fourth formers are at the most difficult periods of their adolescent development. Overt activity may be inconsistent with preoccupation with their own insecurities.[8] Young adolescent groups will obviously not be the best advertisements for community schools while people judge on criteria of involvement with academic and similar work. But then probably any group, teachers and other adults included, will appear pretty inactive when left to themselves.

(ii) In our situation in particular, we selected a high proportion of non-academically minded children and an extremely high proportion of children with very deep and serious problems in their backgrounds. At least seven of our children need individual therapy and attention and another five have serious family problems. One fourth former literally cannot read any but the simplest words and three others have reading problems of extreme urgency. All these children need a very supportive environment and we have had some success despite our lack of permanent staff. Maybe an increase in numbers up to about fifty would provide a more balanced outcome. I am not saying we should be without these children, but that if one has mostly these children one's immediate aims must be considerably changed. One thing to notice is that we had a predominantly native Australian intake in an area heavily saturated with migrants. Australians still living in the area, given a general desire to move elsewhere, may have some particular characteristics.[9]

(iv) We also probably started off in the wrong way. Our initial policy of excusions to get to know each other quite possibly resulted in the children expecting the teachers to provide the entertainment and when we refused to do any more, in the hope that they would develop things for themselves, they felt the more lost as a result.

Community school children with different backgrounds, from other age groups and in somewhat different circumstances, *have* been observed to be self-initiating and active, both academically and practically. We need to work out more how to achieve this in our situation and this year seems to have given some strong indications. They have got to be put to the test.

Other problems. The lack of academic activity has obviously worried a lot of parents and caused some withdrawals of children from the cottage. This is very understandable and a lot more contact with parents would have been desirable.[10] We started off well, but due to a lot of incidental problems neither the Educational Task Force member nor I could put in the time to keep up this side of the project. I consider this a major failing.

Some reflections

There is a theoretical problem underneath some of the previous discussion which I have not yet seen my way through. It arises insofar as it seems to me that it is important for children to develop an ability to initiate activity for themselves and equally important for them to be faced with extending and socially confrontive situations in order that they may come to understand the realities better. But it is not the case that self-initiating children will choose to involve themselves in important situations.

In a long-term community school, I would have no qualms about pressuring children into what I consider important experiences, because it seems this would be reconcilable with enough free activity not to endanger the development of independence in the children. However, in school situations where the children have had their school lives organised for them for so long, their reaction in our situation has been to accept organisation fairly readily, but at the expense of having to face up to independent and personal decisions. Under these circumstances does one refuse to organise and hope for eventual breakthrough while letting slip the aspect of placing them in socially informative situations or does one let slip the independence? It's very hard to find a middle road and it's complicated further in that activity in the social world is so much more informative when self-initiated. If organised by teachers it is too easily treated as just another school activity.

It may be worthwhile to mention something of our experience with teachers, parents and employers. I can see no way to combat the hostile reactions of some teachers but we found that it was not difficult to persuade most teachers to approve the starting of the project. The most persuasive argument was to suggest that we would take a proportion of their 'difficult' children. In the community school the difficult children are not necessarily the children who are difficult in the normal school.

Parents, on the other hand, were impressed by arguments of relevance; i.e. they themselves seemed to see the usual school programme as largely irrelevant to anything but qualifications, so they appreciated examples of activity with job situations etc. However, most parents seemed to be unaware of the implications of the abolition of external exams before the sixth form and hence were worried about the lack of prescribed subject work. Even when the implications were explained they remained troubled deep down. A number seemed happy that their children had had the year during which they had seen them mature and open out but not to allow them another year of the same. It was time, in their view, to get on with achievement of qualifications, even when, in fact, there simply are no qualifications to gain but attendance – this they did not seem prepared to grasp.

The employers were on the whole quite encouraging and we talked to them about the need for liaison between employers and the school and the irrelevance of most school experience for job training. The most serious danger to relations with employers may come from employers not getting their information on community schools from close experience with a school but from the innuendos of even the most favourable press articles.[11] It is so easy to create a scare in their minds. Some employers of course would have nothing to do with such situations but there seem enough that will. Eventually we will probably have to rely on trade union support for a satisfactory extension of possiblities.

Prospects

School A, partly under the influence of the cottage development, has decided to adopt a horizontal staff structure in the school as far as practicable; i.e. teachers will be assigned as much as possible to a form level and hence to one group of children. This will increase the flexibility of their situation and begin to approach the community school situation with some of their groups.

Despite heavy attacks on the cottage from some teachers, the principal has suggested that the project be extended next year to include fifty children from the school. This should do much to remedy some faults that have earlier been discussed.

Together with other community schools, we have stimulated considerable interest in the idea and in programmes which are now being operated in Melbourne. Our teachers have spoken of the community school situation to numerous parent and teacher groups. This is no more true than for the

Educational Task Force member who has taken on so much of the responsibility.

The cottage has provided an invaluable experience for a number of students in initial training over the past year. There will have been twelve who had substantial experience in the situation. There have also been a large number of visitors from other teacher training institutions than La Trobe's School of Education and interest continues to grow.

Finally I would hope that next year will see a situation where the cottage will take on less of the flavour of an annexe or mere attachment and will become just a part of the school — albeit an independent and different part. There seems little future in community schools merely as annexes.

9. *School and community: the link with parents*

Team One

Much in the immediately preceding chapters makes it clear that, in schools of the inner-city, it would be difficult not to be sharply aware of the influences outside the school which affect the behaviour and performance of children in the classroon. It is equally clear that the Educational Task Force Project further emphasised the importance of these influences, in particular that of the home background.

The courses of study undertaken by the teacher-students who formed task force teams did much to confirm experience in emphasising the primacy of this factor but now the teams began to notice that a considerable volume of literature attributed to schools the same sort of self-imposed isolation and lack of practical impact that is quite commonly thought to be the fault with Departments of Education or universities. One member of Team One suddenly woke up to the fact that school may so impress the parents with their own social incompetence that it becomes a place to be avoided.[1]

For a long time the matter of parent–teacher and home–school interaction ran through seminars and discussions concerned with work done in other directions. It was a constantly recurring theme, cropping up first in this context and then in that. As the team began increasingly to feel the need to work together on a joint endeavour[2] and to consider what this should be, parent contact began to present itself as an issue not properly to be dealt with incidentally but in its own right. It was therefore adopted.

School attitudes to parents. Having made this decision the team devoted its reading to the issue and, in consultation with the project director, decided upon a third term component for the core course of the Educational Task Force project which would provide a basis for an exploration of home–school relations with special reference to the convergence or divergence of parent and teacher attitudes to educational issues.[3] Enough had already been read and discussed for a number of important points to have become clear. Among them were that how a school sees itself in relation to parents is an indicator of the nature of its relation to the community it serves and also of the view held of the professional educator and his role.

120

The work of the Hillview Project of the University of Bristol impressed the team at this time. The account given by Hannam and his associates effectively stresses the value of out of school contact between teachers, parents and children.[4] Much that they say echoes the opinion expressed by Midwinter.

So much is known of the imbalance of home and school in socially different areas that it becomes imperative to take a step or two towards the parents ... If we believe in the need for a harmony of interest between school and home ... then it is urgently necessary to harmonize the culture and values between them.[5]

The team decided to place a literal interpretation upon the phrase 'a step or two towards the parents' and to take themselves out of the school situation and into parent territory, so to speak, presenting themselves as persons who happened to be teachers rather than advancing upon parents concealing the person behind the shield of the professional role.

There were obvious reasons for this decision, some of the most important of which are mentioned in the preceding chapters. The migrant parent is frequently at a loss in handling the bureaucracies of a strange and complicated society. When dealing with its representatives he therefore strains to please and to comply particularly when he is within the official spaces of these agencies. He strives to say 'the right thing', which is by no means what he might actually have in mind or wish to say if it was 'proper' to do so. However kind, willing to explain, or ready to listen the teacher in school might be when talking with parents it remains possible, even probable, that the teacher will appear to the parent as the entrenched official, securely authoritative, invested with something of the mystique of professionalism that Goffman describes. The impression upon the parent is: 'that the licensed practitioner is someone who has been reconstituted by his learning experience and is now set apart from other men'.[6] It is not necessary for the teacher to wish it to be this way, nor is the impression inevitably dispelled when it is not wished for by the teacher.

The team wanted to discover what was actually in the minds of parents concerning their children's education in School A. To do so it seemed that they must reverse the order of things, put themselves at risk beyond the sheltered situation of the school and be *seen* to have discarded the mantle of authority. The proposed approach did not commit them to abandonment of their own professional judgement or expertise. It would be left open whether what was in the mind of the parent turned out to be either feasible or desirable. On the other hand it did not demand that the parent deliver himself up to the teacher and discouraged the idea that this was what was happening. The aim would be to minimise the risk that the parent would feel he was being told what was desirable under conditions which made it politic for him to accept and agree.

In forming this intention the team had to consider just what relation of school to community it implied. What might be called the fortress-cum shop concept of the school must be abandoned. This concept has had application almost from the beginning of popular education. Many pioneers in the cause of education for all urged that what had been handed *on* from generation to generation of the privileged minority in society should now be handed *down* to the children of those who had hitherto been excluded. Schools were opened, the children of the ordinary man ushered in, the gates closed against the ignorance without and the children enjoined to partake of the mysteries denied their parents.

In essence the model is paternalistic and directive. It has not yet been whole-heartedly rejected despite all the curriculum reforms and changes in teaching method that have occurred and all the extension of schooling opportunities. By its operation parents remain irremediable cases, not only beyond benefit themselves but also not capable of contributing anything of value about curriculum and teaching for their children. It is observable that many parents accept this still, particularly those of humble occupational status as were the Southern European migrants in the areas served by Schools A and B.[1] They accept that they will be invited (summoned) to the school as a body from time to time but that there are quite definite limits to what will be discussed. As Goodacre remarks: '(P)arental suggestions about curriculum, teaching methods, staff appointments, etc . . . are unthinkable.'[8] Sociological research into social role relationships in education have shown this attitude to be encouraged by many teachers, generally tacitly but sometimes quite specifically.[9] The team in School A were given an actual instance in one of their core course seminars. A senior member of the staff of a school which had been built to operate on the open plan principle had been invited to consult with the team on the problems and disadvantages of the open classroom (its merits being assumed). In the course of the seminar the matter of parent opinion was raised. The visitor commented that once the school's programme and its rationale had been explained, questions invited and so on, there was little more to be done if the parent still did not understand or agree with what was going on; it was, after all, the best and most advanced of educational practice and could not be obstructed. There was no arrogance or disrespect intended here. This able and sincere teacher admitted that it was indeed probable that many parents were out of sympathy with the carefully thought out work of the school and that this was sad indeed. But no more could be done: that was how things were. Yet the discussion had revealed that the parents did have ideas about curriculum and teaching. Was it really 'unthinkable' that they should be seriously considered, not as objections to something else but as views backed by reasons? Plainly the parents were not sure why this should be so but felt impotent against the professionals. The result did not accord with Midwinter's talk of a need for 'harmony of interest between home and school' but it did speak of the imbalance between the two that 'is so injurious'.[10] Was this consistent with the best?

School A itself was not totally without some manifestations of the same attitude. As the staff became aware of the intentions of the team some drew attention to the wealth of information that could be obtained merely by recourse to the school's records. 'Parent nights' were mentioned as highly successful occasions productive of close contacts with parents. It was pointed out that the school made it known to parents that they could make an appointment to see someone at the school whenever they had any worries or anxieties about their children. In short, the school made great efforts to know about the parents and to understand them. A case study approach was always in operation at staff meetings in respect of 'problem children'; children with adverse home circumstances. There was active consultation with the Psychology and Guidance Branch in connection with the disadvantaged.

All of which was very true and very much more than many a school can claim. The time and effort expended and the sympathetic professional care taken, told of a staff with a commitment to human values. Much was gained by the pupils in terms of intellectual and personal welfare as a consequence and much done for the peace of mind of their parents. Nevertheless, there was about it all something of the restrictiveness of application which McGeeney remarks upon. He notices the narrowness of context allowed for parent–teacher contact; the way in which interaction is focussed upon the child of the parent and rarely includes discussion of general principles governing curriculum and aims.[11] As in the usual case so in School A. There was the fixed schedule of occasions when parents came to the school as a body. Beyond this, interaction of a face to face kind seemed occasioned only by crisis. A child's failure to progress or his seriously unsatisfactory behaviour might cause the parent sufficient concern for him to seek an interview or the school to invite him to one.

Is this the way things should be? When a parent says that he is going to the school but not to some formal function, is his visit to be thought of as justified if, and only if, there are grounds for believing something is wrong? Why should it be that the individual who is a parent relates to the school only as a child producer and 'owner'? There may be something odd about visiting a dentist when there is nothing wrong with one's teeth, but is the situation of the school in the community directly comparable? The team had arrived at a point of suspended judgement on these issues.

The questions were not merely 'theoretical'; pleasantly stimulating items for seminar discussions and all very well for that. Had they been so emasculated in importance then much less attention might have been given to the team's deliberations than was actually the case in the school. At least some staff were not completely happy that the team proposed to make external contacts with parents in the service of seeking to arrive at conclusions to fit the questions. Some felt that parents might be alarmed, others that the parents not contacted might feel left out, others still that there was a danger that the child–teacher relationship might be prejudiced somehow. There was a certain opinion that nothing could be discovered that wasn't already known.

It behoved the team to receive these worries seriously as the judgements of people quite as concerned with sound educational practice as they themselves were. The problem was that simple recourse to fact does nothing to settle things one way or another. Parents might be alarmed by exploratory visits if school and the teacher are allowed to have the same aura as the law and the policeman. The unvisited parent may feel 'left out' if the teacher goes to the parent only as a special privilege. This depends entirely upon what school sets out to be to the community. The debate is upon what ought to be rather than upon how things actually are.[12]

The team set against the objections offered, the findings which have been mentioned in the foregoing together with many more, including that of the Plowden Report's survey of schools and parents to the effect that about fifty per cent of the English parents included in the investigation would have liked to know more about their children's schooling and (more apposite still), about a third thought that teachers did not know enough about the children they taught.[13] The Hillview project underlined the last point and encouraged students to make extensive contact with the child outside the school, including visits to the home to talk with the parents. Although not always a comfortable experience the workers in the project found that it improved and strengthened the teacher–child relationship within the school.[14]

The team therefore decided to brave the difficulties and to approach some parents on their own ground, seeking to establish a parity of associational status with them from which might be gleaned a clearer picture of parental attitudes to school and to educational issues. Of course, a wholesale invasion of homes was never thought of as anything but both undesirable and impractical. Some limited case study work seemed both feasible and desirable. Teachers stand in danger of becoming insulated agents within the institution of school when they travel in from their homes in other parts of the city, occupy themselves in classrooms through the day, then travel back again to their homes in distant and different suburbs, to mark, prepare for the next day and, perhaps, read about parents of the inner-city. In the extreme case they can become remote from the life of the neighbourhood of the school to an extent which makes of them what Bryson and Thompson refer to as external caretakers.

Caretakers are classified as 'internal' or 'external' not on a geographical basis but according to two criteria-whether or not the caretaker comes from a similar social situation and whether or not he shares the values of those to whom he offers (his services).[15]

The same writers point out that there are difficulties of communication between external caretakers and the community arising from the different interpretations each makes of the same situation. While nothing could put the team in the position of the migrant parents they could at least do something to discover what values were held by them. Whether they could share them was another matter again.

By the time the team was ready to embark upon its programme of parent contact some work had been done by the project director on the lines suggested by the McLeish study of attitudes to education.[16] Measures of tough mindedness, formalism and radicalism regarding educational issues had been taken in respect of a group of some sixty parents in areas about the inner city. No more than face value could safely be lent to the results but, once this was understood, there was something of interest to be found in a comparison between these results and the results obtained from a group of nearly one hundred teachers in schools in the city. Between the two groups there was a systematic difference in attitude, the teachers being less tough minded and formalistic than the parents, the parents being less radical in their views than the teachers. When the results for the parent group were compared with those for a second group of teachers, this time the eighty-four applicants for the two task force teams, the difference was of the same nature but was more marked, and this was also true when the teachers compared were the staffs of the two schools A and B.[17]

Viewing the results with all caution they still encourage certain suspicions. If one takes the responses made to certain of the schedule items by the parents in comparison with the responses to the same items made by the teacher groups mentioned above and allows that the parent group was not totally unrepresentative, then the following dichotomies become real possibilities. Where Schools A and B found the practice of giving marks and

125

issuing class positions to be inappropriate as educational practice, the parents might well feel the opposite to be true. Where the schools maximised individual work, the parents might well wish to see common instruction for all in specific subjects. Where the schools felt that children should work co-operatively the parents might see it to be fitting that each child should be judged on his own unaided efforts.[18]

An opposition of attitudes in much these terms was thought to be just what did exist in many cases by the staff of School A. (Hence the query as to what the team thought it would discover that was at all new.) The point to be made here is that the staff's realisation was, for many, an end to the matter; it was not a matter for action so much as a fact of educational life. Such a view is entirely compatible with the fortress-cum shop concept of school.

By this time the team in School A had gained enough understanding of the school as a social system to know that change is not effected through mere dialectic and the dispassionate weighing of pros and cons in public discussion. It must go quietly about its chosen task, seeking to avoid any of the undesirable consequences feared by the staff, hoping that, by so doing, it would dispel any feeling that extended parent contact threatened the school. One does not change the ruling concepts of a group by bull-dozing them down as one might assault an actual fortress. In the last analysis change of concept is a function of the possessor of the concept; other people can do no more than invite discussion and review by structuring situations which encourage change.

Results of the investigation. The purpose of the work was admirably expressed in a term paper by one of the team members.

A comment in the Plowden Report on the results of Parent Teacher Association activities, where parents and teachers worked together in a situation in which the parents were at least as competent as the teachers (suggests that), Goodacre is correct when she says that, without *social* contact and the relationships so formed, parents and teachers think of each other in stereotyped terms.[19] This thought was in our minds when we decided to gain first hand experience of what parent attitudes were to the school and hoped to discover some way of creating positive and closer relationships – particularly with migrant families.

After consultation with a most helpful and skilled member of the Psychology and Guidance Branch of the Department of Education, further and equally valuable guidance from Professor Jean Martin of the School of Social Science at La Trobe University, the team set about its field work. One of the staff who was of the nationality of the predominant migrant group in the area freely gave her services as an interpreter and this was of incalculable assistance. For this aspect of the Educational Task Force work she virtually became one of the team.

The general plan was to seek interviews with parents through the agency of their children and by letter, explaining that the team was anxious for first hand interchange with parents. The team worked hard to construct an approach which would allow the parent to voice his views freely over what was hoped would be a series of three interviews with each. The parents chosen were selected on as near a random basis as made sense. (It did *not* seem sensible to approach parents of children with whom no member of the team had had contact nor to approach parents of children with special difficulties. Parents known to be atypically supportive or hostile were also avoided.)

It is not necessary to detail the data gained except in terms of general points. These were as follows:

(1) In most cases it was found that the parent did not have a clear idea of the rationale which informed the school's work and was unclear why it was that children did not sit in serried ranks to be 'taught their lessons'.

(2) The system of progress reports of a discursive nature, given and discussed on parent nights, did not provide the parent with information that was entirely meaningful to him. At the back of many a parent's mind there lurked the question, 'Does this mean eighty per cent or ten per cent or what?'

(3) The majority of parents interviewed felt some uncertainty as to whether the children were sufficiently supervised outside the classroom. They saw the proprieties of general behaviour and deportment to be the province of the teacher.

(4) Parents found the teachers' approach to their charges to be sometimes strange. Here the reference was to the extent of informal contact in the school, where teacher and children laughed and joked and 'disrespectful' comments were not unknown.

(5) The parents almost unanimously wished that their children had more rigidly specified homework to do, e.g. set exercises from a common text book.

(6) Many parents would have liked to help their children in their work at home, but, apart from taking care that time was provided and used for homework, they were prevented by their own level of education, including their difficulties with the English language, and by lack of understanding of what was required of the child.

(7) Parents wished to see their children 'go as far as possible' in their education. They found it very difficult to characterise what they meant by

this except in terms of job possibility. Many parents had worked or were still working extremely hard in two, sometimes three, jobs in order to buy their houses, purchase their own shops, or simply because their own skills and recognised qualifications were such that well paid employment was difficult to obtain. In their countries of origin the educated man and the secure man were synonymous. Many had come to Australia because they saw no way to *obtain this security for their children in their own countries.*[20]

(8) None of the parents were actively hostile to the school or in any doubt about the goodwill of the staff. They were aware of the difficulties and problems the school had encountered and were ready to help in any way they could.

The points may be illustrated by the following excerpts from reports of the interviews by various members of the team.

(i) When asked why (parent thought his children) did not work at school he said that his boys did not prepare lessons at home nor were they able to explain the lessons they had done at school to him.

(ii) (At Saturday School) children would learn a lesson that the teacher set, would recite it to him (the parent) and then to the teacher next time. If unable to do this they would be required to do the lesson again.

(iii) (The parent said) that teachers are too lax with the children and that children in Australia did not fear or respect teachers ... He said that in (country of origin) teachers *were* feared and respected ... and dropped one's mark by 3–4 points if one did not behave. He mentioned that (his child) did well at school there and received 8/10.

(iv) The family decided to migrate for financial reasons. As (parent) said, 'With four children, what else could I do?'

(v) Neither parent completed Primary School. Neither parent knows much English.

New moves. It was clear enough from all this that some dichotomy or imbalance of view did exist between at least some parents and the school. It is also quite unfair to discount the parents' views as irresponsible or totally unreasonable even if it would be false to assert that they were altogether wise. Many of the points above did seem to indicate that much might be gained from some move to what might be called 'parent education', provided that that term was rigorously purged of all suggestion of patronage or intention to propagate infallible educational dogma. How this could be achieved was another thing again, requiring, in the first instance, an approach to the school staff. The team now turned its attention to these issues. Once again excerpts from their own papers serve well to describe the strategies adopted.

Concerning the parents. Whilst, on the whole, parents seemed anxious to talk to someone – particularly someone from the school itself – about the child's life at school and about factors that are of concern to them, there is an inevitable cooling off and let down when they realise that no change or action is definitely forthcoming.

The major task of explaining some of School A's procedures is made very difficult with migrants who have been brought up in a very rigid and authoritarian school system and whose adherence to the traditional has been strengthened by fear and anxiety in an alien society.

Concerning the team. For us at School A it would seem that our first task now is to inform the staff in general of our findings. This ... would be best done informally by each of us making as much contact with our colleagues as possible.

Little has been done so far in Australia by way of exploring new avenues of home–school relations. The time is ripe for innovation but ... without the concern, interest and participation of all of the staff, any attempts at achieving more meaningful parent–school relations would be fruitless. The question of what can/should be done is a matter for the whole staff.

We should share what we are learning with the rest of the staff. One thing that could be done would be to distribute documents of the following kind.

(a) A summary of the literature on contact with parents outlining the social and educational activities which have proved successful elsewhere in gaining parental interest, co-operation, school participation and parent education.

(b) A document outlining local 'research' in regard to parents. We now know of a number of schools which are developing various sorts of approach on an 'experimental' basis.

(c) A summary or extracts from *An Australian New town*[21] which may point out the problem of external caretaking to us all.

Concerning action by the school. Some suggestions which might be considered at staff meetings are as follows.

(a) *Group discussions with parents.* Teachers would need some training in the psychology of groups and of the function of anxiety in the conduct of groups.

(b) *School meetings.* Discussion of specific issues; e.g. wearing of uniform, curriculum design.

These should involve hearing *both* sides of the case.

(c) *Panel discussions.* Follow these with small group discussion of problems. Have *parent* leaders.

(d) *Informal contacts.* What kind? It is probably a matter of individual decision.

(e) *Meetings in homes.* Some 'key' parents who are influential in the neighbourhood and interested in education in general may co-operate here.

(f) *Casual school visits.* Parents should be able to observe the school in action; i.e. about its day to day work.

(g) *Education shops and neighbourhood exhibitions.* As described in Midwinter's *Social Environment and the Urban School.*

Towards the end of the third term a staff meeting instructed the team to bring suggestions for making a more thorough survey of parent opinion. Upon its outcomes the staff would then explore the need for extending school–home relationships. The team was thus presented with a further task to take into the second year of its operation in the school which held the promise of inspiring an innovative move from the staff as a whole. It was reasonable to feel that some change in the climate of opinion had been brought about and that the Educational Task Force was becoming the instrument it was intended to be. What was most encouraging was that the team had been given an evaluative task to do to add to its schedule of 'practical' objectives.

Team Two

School B's approach to the issue of parent–school contact and participation was quite different from that of School A. The brief that awaited the second team directed it to evaluate the school's assumptions about parents, together with the appropriateness and effectiveness of its relation with them. In the preliminary sessions the principal of School B was ready to say that her own knowledge of parent attitudes and life styles was inadequate. This is not to say that she admitted to any lack of care and effort in comparison with anyone else and any such assertion would be blatantly false. Instead, it marks the school's realisation of how much needed to be done and the scarcity of knowledge about how it should be done.

If anything the southern European ethnic group which dominated the area of School B was less well endowed with educational qualifications than that predominant in the area of School A and came from a more rigidly stratified society. Secondly the social roles of males and females were more sharply differentiated. Where the male adolescent was considered to have a free and exploratory social life as if by right, the female adolescent was to be protected from exploitation and preserved in virgin innocence until marriage. The male parent was thought of as having a role to play in public affairs; the female's role was strongly influential but essentially domestic. She exercised influence upon affairs in the community through her influence in the family. In matters of the home she was accorded managerial status by her husband and owed obedience by her children.

Migration to Australia involved a translation from a rural community which was generally tightly confined, to an urban situation on the northern European pattern with all its tolerance of difference and deviance of values, behaviour and general life style. It came as a shock to many migrant parents that their children readily accepted ways and customs other than those of the family and the country of origin. The parents' own experience had been of life in a parochial situation which held conditions stable over the generations. Chains of migration were built out of this context, one family drawing another after it, assisting the latest comer to settle in the same areas as itself, fostering a greater belief that the same social cohesion and confinement would persist as in the village left behind than the facts would warrant.

There was a high incidence of poverty among the migrant families and poverty in an affluent society of an industrial nature, where there is a high incidence of social mobility, is quite a different thing from poverty in a village where few are much above a subsistence standard of living.[22] In the latter situation the stability of the family is not threatened in the same way as poverty appears to undermine stability and cohesion in the modern city, where lack of means is taken to be a mark of incompetence.

Family distress and disruption have inevitable repercussions upon the child's school performance and behaviour. In School B, professional concern merged with common humanity to dictate the school's declared policy of acting as an intermediary between the damaged family and those agencies able to assist – departments of social welfare, free hospitals and so on. In this school, with its all girl population and seventy per cent saturation of migrant children from families where the daughter is traditionally assistant to the main prop and authority in matters domestic, it was found that migration could bring about a drastic alteration in role effectiveness and even in role playing. In dealing with institutions the mother was more at a loss than anywhere else. The daughter was more conversant with the language and the institutions of the new country – after all the school sought to make her so.

Where help for the family necessitated contact with the mother and the compilation of a case, it often transpired that the only acceptable translator to the mother was the daughter. No-one else would be trusted to convey intimate family details. Further to this, the mother would listen to no-one else when the principal found it necessary to have explained that such agencies as were just mentioned must be visited. If the mother was persuaded she then often put the whole affair into the hands of the daughter from that point; in crisis the mother leaned upon the daughter and the latter directed her.

Experience of families in crisis aroused the school's suspicion that it may generally be the case among migrant families in the area that the fate of the family hinged more upon the daughter than upon the mother, that the former advised, informed and even instructed the latter in those aspects of living in the society which involved direct dealings with the institutions which served it. Yet the mother must somehow maintain her status and her domestic function, a difficult thing to do when the daughter must be relied upon to provide the 'know how' of living in respect of the workings of the society: especially difficult once crisis created a pressing desire for external assistance.[23] Failure must obviously be damaging to the mother's morale. That was, in its turn, dangerous for the child. A tension was introduced at the nerve centre of the family; in its internal relationships.

As has been previously remarked the team for School B were involved in an extensive series of meetings over almost half a year before officially being placed upon School B's staff. From the middle of the term before that event, the team was virtually engaged upon its brief, meeting regularly at the school with key staff, the principal, the project director and his colleague. It was therefore functioning as a dynamic and integrated unit well before the beginning of its two-year secondment. In much the same way the Educational Task Force *course* for this team was really embarked upon from late September rather than in the following March, the official beginning of the academic year for B.Ed students.

In respect of the tasks concerning home and school relations given the team in its brief,[24] the team proposed the following in active association with the people above mentioned.

(1) Each member had assigned to him some thirty pupils as a 'home group'. With the assistance of some research personnel procured by use of a grant to the Educational Task Force project made by the Myer Foundation, each of the team would undertake a piece of practical research into home conditions and parental attitudes on the same lines as the work done by the team in School A but working to a more controlled design and over a longer period. This would be carried through in liaison with the member of the

Psychology and Guidance Section of the Department of Education who assisted by acting in a consultant capacity to Team One. Certain others of the staff of School B would also take part in the work.

(2) The team would set up a council of parents. This body would be invited to assist in facilitating the programme of general studies to be designed and carried through by the team and two other staff. The programme would be for the children whose parents would be both the focus of the study described in (1) and from whom the parent council would be formed.

Membership of the council would be enlarged periodically to allow of a greater number to serve.

(3) The team possessed the linguistic expertise which would enable them to present much material in their general studies programme in the native language of the prevailing migrant group. Parents would be encouraged to help their children with their work at home.

(4) Use would be made of the local newspaper published in the migrant's native language. Children's work on appropriate topics would be submitted. Use would also be made of such local shops and similar establishments as would feature exhibitions of children's work. It would be one of the parent council's functions to seek these outlets.

(5) Topics in the general studies programme would include aspects of living in cities with special reference to the area about the school in the first case and then to the city of Melbourne in general. The parent council and all parents of the children involved would be encouraged to assist in arranging visits, work experiences etc.

The last four of these proposals have specific reference to the problem of parental insecurity of grasp upon the management of social institutions. Secondly they cast this consideration into the context of the education of the children, the school's primary task. There are prudential limits to the extent to which teachers can venture into active intervention in family affairs; they must not engage themselves in areas of work for which they are ill equipped and where they may do more harm than good.[25] The danger is avoided if the basis for action remains the children and their school careers, a basis which still leaves open a considerable range of activity in respect of parents and homes; for example, the first proposal entails considerable preliminary study and skill acquisition of a non-didactic nature but is directly relevant to the school careers of the children.

If one compares the programme outlined above with the schedule of suggestions Team One brought to the staff of School A after their first stage investigation,[26] it will be seen that there are close similarities. The first moves of Team Two were to be the subsequent moves of Team One. In part this was undoubtedly attributable to the larger preparation time afforded the second team and to the placement procedure adopted to accommodate them in the school. The first fact testifies eloquently to the validity of the contention by the Chicago Ford Training and Placement Programme that teachers who are appointed to a school should not have to make first acquaintance with each other and the school on the first day of the term, at which time everyone must *begin* the business of social and professional orientation and integration. Concerning the placement strategy adopted in School B it will be recalled that there was a foreseen risk that the concentration of the team as a group in the school might cause them to be seen as a faction isolated from the rest of the staff.[27] The degree of staff interaction with the group over the months prior to the team's official entry into the school, all but eliminated this danger and, at the same time, welded the group into a coherent unit which was realistically adjusted to the school and eager to go to work there.

However, it would be dangerous to say that School B was at a more advanced stage of thinking and operation than Schoool A and that this explains the differences between the careers of the two teams. What goes on in one school as opposed to another is a function of a complex web of influences and circumstances peculiar to the particular school so that the pattern of educational evolution of one school will differ from that of another.[28] It is this that makes prior orientation and careful placement an essential to efficiency.

PART 3

Evaluations; unfinished tasks

Introductory comments

Perspective

The idea of the Educational Task Force project is not one which has a finite goal so specific that, when reached, a terminal point has been attained. The second stage of the project, the placing of a team in School B, was informed by the lessons learnt from the experience with School A and Team One. Consideration of both these together provides a fuller and a different picture than consideration of either one alone or by mere comparison the one with the other. And so it can go on.

This is particularly true for the understanding of what is involved in a social systems approach to the training and education of teacher-students and the intimately related concern of learning about the career of innovative procedures in schools. In respect of the last concern what becomes increasingly clear is that it is a brave man who will predict what will happen without a careful and participatory study of the particular people and the particular school in which it is proposed to bring about some change. Given this study in any one case, it then becomes clear that work of the kind undertaken by the University of Chicago Ford Training and Placement Programme and the Educational Task Force project at La Trobe University can equip people with a procedural knowledge and a social insight which greatly increases their potentiality as effective instruments of innovation. They become more resilient and flexible because they have come to see things in terms of process. Even if they can make no certain prognostications as to just what will come about, their insight is into *how* things come about. To an extent it is fair to say that what they gain is the capacity to live with uncertainty without surrendering responsibility or abdicating from the role of originator.

Towards a balanced view

Accounts of projects such as the Educational Task Force, when given by those who mount them, are prone to omit those things which tarnish the sheen of success. We have striven to avoid the fault but the task is not complete as yet and the following chapter seeks to remedy this.

At least over its first year the team in School A failed to bring into the arena of action one consideration which greatly pre-occupied it as being of urgent necessity. However, it is vital to understand that what is to be discussed cannot be properly treated as a failure in any sense but that one thing it seemed necessary to do was not accomplished and must be tackled again but differently.

Tolerance of 'failure' taken in this sense is part of the learning that is necessary to teacher–students: ability to tolerate it is one of the reasons why it is essential to operate in groups of mutually supportive people. When something presses upon one as an essential task but its achievement is resisted by others having an equally strong but opposite conviction, the tension set up is probably very much to the good in terms of ensuring an evolutionary situation as opposed to a non-negotiable revolutionary or reactionary one. But the isolated individual who can hold to this rather than opting out into acquiescence is a rare one, and the person who can both hold and prevail is rarer still. Even a group requires all the strength its internal support can provide when the issue bites deep; when it matters. Yet it is vital to preserve the evolutionary situation rather than allow the flacidity of unconvinced acceptance to rule, for the latter is but a step from the non-negotiable exercise of power that is the essence of the two situations contrasted above with evolutionary one.

Thus we return to the points made in the early chapters of the book. Having done so it is worth reiterating that the discussion is of people, of teachers, as they are in general and not of atypical cases or of those with less of some desirable attribute than most of us. (If anything the case is that the people involved have rather more of such attributes than most but remain as blessedly like most of us to tell of the usual rather than the odd.)

Summary

In recounting this, as in much of Part 2 of the book, evaluation will accompany description and analysis. However, the final chapter will attempt to contribute something more to the specific question, 'What can the project achieve?.

We can ask how, in their view, the teacher-students have benefited from this form of advanced course in Education and how their results, their academic grades, show any indication of benefit. It has already been indicated that there is evidence to show that their academic work was brought to bear upon their work in school.

We should also inquire whether the project has sufficient potential for further development or whether its essential form consists of placing teams in one school or another, in itself a not inconsiderable aspect but perhaps not the only possibility. Finally we must see whether the project has gained enough support beyond the University to make such possibilities, if they exist, a reality.

10. The open classroom: taboos and invitations

School A

At the end of Team One's first year in their school, a teachers' organisation and some members of the La Trobe School of Education held a two day seminar at the university, a member of Team One being a principal speaker. The subject of the seminar was the open classroom. The intention of the organisers was that ideas be shared, problems discussed and some account given of what was going on in schools throughout Victoria. It was a laudable enterprise which was very well attended, produced lively discussions upon excellent lead papers and put many teachers in touch with ideas they found to be exciting and valuable.

Yet, as was remarked earlier, although the university may be the central and vital arena for the meeting of minds, the making of plans and the construction of solutions, it is not the place where improvements are actually made nor where problems are cleared away.[1] That place is the school. Getzels points out that the meeting ground of the university is an artificial or contrived one.[2] From the experiences of the Chicago Ford Training and Placement Programme and the Educational Task Force project itself, one may add that the mark of its artificiality is its lack of the social dynamics which influence everything that occurs in the school situation.

Before what emerges from occasions such as the seminar can be said to have anything but a potential utility it must be translated into processes tailored to the particular school. That requires action in the school. One of the ironies is that what the seminar was doing over its two days of deliberation, namely following Ginsberg in examining the open classroom situation in order to resolve its difficulties and set right its imperfections,[3] Team One had sought to do in School A for over a year without succeeding to any member's satisfaction. It is entirely in keeping with the intentions of the Educational Task Force project and in the interests of an effective meshing of theory and practice that this should be explained. We must not interpret Getzels' paper[4] to discount all need for the 'artificial' meeting ground, nor, by default, allow what eventuates upon this ground to be emasculated by such a lack of practical implementation as could come about when this sort of 'failure' occurs.

140

The team sought to involve itself in an issue of evaluation rather than innovation in this instance. It will be remembered that Team One's initial brief differed from that of Team Two precisely in that the first lacked any evaluative task. The fact began to have more and more significance as time went on. The team in School A had carried through some valuable innovative tasks but now that it had suggested an examination of the efficiency of the school's open classroom organisation it inspired a potentially destructive clash of interests which could have prejudiced any further work, innovative or otherwise.

Basically the issue was whether one should question the way the general studies programme was carried through under a system where teachers worked together in groups of three in association with eighty to ninety children gathered in a single large room. The team *did* wish to question this but encountered stern opposition to such probing. In dealing with this situation the team, together with the project director, acquired a real understanding of the factors affecting their relations with the rest of the school. Theoretical studies in a removed situation stand subordinate to these influences at the best of times, but when one seeks to employ knowledge and techniques so gained without due recognition or in the face of deep seated beliefs which stand in opposition to one's efforts, there is little or no hope of success and a great risk that damage will be done.

What matters in this case is the source of the opposition encountered by the team, for not all groups within a staff are in a position of holding power or exerting wide influence upon the opinion of the others. It is therefore important to identify which staff were principally concerned to oppose the Educational Task Force in their efforts to probe the open classroom in School A.

An examination of the records of staff membership reveals that a mere eleven per cent of the total staff strength consisted of teachers who were in the school at the time when the need for urban renewal in the area produced the activity which included a plan for a new kind of school. (See chapter 3.) Over the five or so years from that point in time to the time of the Educational Task Force's entry into the school, only the principal and that tiny number of the total staff strength remained the same. As has been described earlier, upon the backs of this minority the school had made its way through a veritable sea of tribulations towards a future as a school with a different way of working from that which it had had prior to the change in the character of the neighbourhood which had included the migrant inflow. They were still piloting the school forward towards the point when it would have a building designed for that new way of working.

Of course, all of this group were either of senior rank in terms of career grades or in positions of influence within the structure of the school; e.g. convenors of general studies teaching teams. Taken as a group then, they represented the 'establishment' within the school.

The hard-line, conservative, or what is perhaps better thought of as the preservative attitude, which was opposed to Team One's effort to secure critical appraisal of the open classroom, was most clearly and forcefully exhibited by the same small number of enduring staff[5] who had worked and were still working in the school through its years of difficult improvisation in temporary accommodation on a temporary site. Only when the new school became a reality could their efforts be fully rewarded. Before that time it was their view that any suggested deficiencies were explained by the adversities of material circumstance being suffered.

The nature of the goal to be attained was by now precisely determined in the sense that plans for the building that was to be the new school had been drawn, approved and passed out for tender. The physical characteristics of the future situation were therefore settled and were totally unsuited to any but the organisation the school had adopted. Any sort of move which might lead to a conclusion that this could be bettered was a frightening one. It prejudiced the hopefulness of the now immutable future rather than bearing upon past or present practice. For a newcomer to point to a defect and assert that it was not the product of circumstance, diminished the validity of belief in the planned future. For a *group* of people – the Educational Task Force – to imagine this could be done was unthinkably menacing. The team must cease its 'complaining' and measure up to the demands of the make-shift situation, not act the sage or the judge.[6] If this line of reasoning lacks something in terms of logic it lacks nothing as a demonstration of the operation of a conservative/preservative attitude or an indication that such an attitude is not tied to a 'traditional' way of doing things.

Comments of the kind quoted from Ginsberg[7], events such as the seminar at La Trobe and the comparatively few schools that have worked on a principle of openness to date, all suggest that it is unlikely that we can safely imagine that we yet have a faultless theoretical model, much less a perfect prototype. On the other hand there is nothing to suggest that what faults there were in School A were of a kind fatal to the concept.

Bearing this in mind we may avoid the error of placing the wrong emphasis upon the tension between Team One and School A. It is unlikely that the best of all possible educational worlds is to be attained in an atmosphere of cosy concensus; indeed, the Educational Task Force project rests upon an assumption that the rigours of social dissonance are to be accepted as an almost inevitable accompaniment and possibly a stimulus to informed initiatives. It was not the tension that was the worry so far as the health of the project was concerned, but that it obstructed open and rational debate for so long.

So far as this one issue is concerned this form of dialogue, with change as an accepted result, has yet to be fully realised. However, the barrier of silence, the imputation of heresy, has been overcome. Towards the end of the third term the staff discussed the possibility of evaluating the open classroom as it was working in the school. In doing so it revived, albeit obliquely, a document from the team which had been 'managed' out of the agenda of a meeting in second term. In this, the team sought to put several questions before the staff as requiring investigation. They included the following:

(i) Does the 'open classroom' as we operate it cater for something more than information gathering? If the answer is affirmative then there is no problem, but if the answer is negative there are two points to be considered. Should we expect children to do more than gather information; if so, how do we ensure that they do so?

(ii) How do we assess and evaluate progress of individuals? We need such information as will check on the success of our programme and to indicate whether the child is working up to his capabilities.

(iii) Do we throw too much responsibility on pupils before they are ready to cope with the enormous demands, both social and intellectual, which a 'free and open' environment makes upon them?[8]

On this second occasion the staff still did not entrust Team One with the task of acting upon these issues as an evaluative instrument in their service, but, nevertheless, there was a recognition that there might be a task to be done. This was a considerable advance. It is, in fact, the only start that leads to anything worth pursuing. What it can lead to is well illustrated by what actually occurred in School B.

School B

Evaluation of the open classroom as it operated in School B was part of Team Two's original brief. Shortly before the team transferred its pre-liminary meetings from the university to the school itself, the project director sat in on a curriculum conference of the staff, during which there was a long and careful debate upon the year's work in the open situation. It was made clear and explicit that many of the problems which Team One wanted to examine in their school were living issues under constant discussion in School B. They were formulated as follows.

(A) Was it really the case that there was greater teacher–pupil and pupil–pupil interaction among eighty to ninety children with three teachers in one large room than between one third of these and one teacher in a 'normal' classroom?

(B) Even when the area was carpeted, tastefully decorated and skilfully furnished, did the space equivalent to three classrooms successfully accommodate the equivalent of three classes when put together, or was a much larger space or a much smaller number of children necessary to efficiency?

(C) To what extent were the objectives of the programme operationally characterised and to what extent were they vague and ambiguous to a point where nothing could count against them?

Opinion among the staff as to what the answers to these questions should be was by no means unanimous but there *was* unanimity that all opinion lacked substantiation at this time.

In the series of meetings between Team Two and staff members which followed this conference, the questions were further discussed in the context of planning for the general studies programme of the year to come. As in the conference, so in these meetings, no one was outright prepared to abandon the principle of openness but everyone recognised that all these queries pointed to the possible need for some modifications to the school's implementation of it. The correct thing to do was to begin by accepting the propositions implicit in the questions. These were:

(a) There could be an increase of purposeful interaction.
(b) A group of eighty or ninety is a large one.
(c) There should be a fairly precise system of assessing progress.

One must then adopt a trial and error approach to find the procedures which increased interaction, reduced group size and yielded more information concerning what had been learnt by the children.

By this time the team was meeting more or less weekly with staff. These considerations were incorporated into their joint discussions over the latter part of the term and the vacation prior to the team's official entry into the school. They influenced the planning of the general studies programme and the content of the core course for the Educational Task Force (which had now become of general interest in the school, the assumption being that most staff would attend for at least fifty per cent of the weekly sessions). When the team began in the school it was agreed that it would work with the established staff to implement the following.

(1) Re. a   The extra-school contact each teacher would make with his

'home group' (see page 132) should be utilised to provide a fuller interaction with the children as well as to establish interaction with the parents.

(2) Re. a and b   Adoption of procedures derived from study of the Philadelphia Project 'School Without Walls'[9] should involve a greater use of the environment as a teaching and learning venue. Children need not be in the classroom – open or otherwise – in order to learn nor should their ventures beyond the school walls be merely a round of visits and excursions.

(3) Re. a and b   Careful examination was to be made of the 'shop hours' restriction of the school's operation. Could it be arranged that some groups and some teachers worked at times outside the traditional and limited span of the school day on some occasions?

(4) Re. c   'Expectancy schedules' of the achievements it was hoped the children would reach would be drawn up. Where what was actually achieved failed to correspond with these then both the programmes of work and the schedules themselves must be subjected to scrutiny.

The composite picture

It is distressingly easy to draw a contrast between the two schools on this issue of the difficulties of running an open classroom. Both schools had adopted a radical organisational idea and both embraced the principle of freedom to learn according to interest and motivation as distinct from learning at the direction of an all knowing authority. However, we find School B to be extending and challenging the Educational Task Force from the beginning by confronting it with realised problems, engaging it in evaluative tasks requiring insight into the workings of the school and charging it to formulate plans which would draw everyone into practical work and theoretical analysis. Team Two, therefore, at the outset of its career stood in a position beyond that reached by Team One after a year of work in its school; School B was correspondingly more progressive in attitude than School A. This is the conclusion to which one is strongly drawn.

Yet it would have been entirely the wrong interpretation to place upon the agreed facts if one was to achieve anything more in School A concerning the open classroom issue. To begin with nothing that has been described allows the conclusion that the actual operation of School A's open classroom was less effective than School B's and no such comparison was made. Secondly, nothing that has been described assumes some monopoly of rectitude for Team One (or Two for that matter). Whether as a team of teacher-students, an individual teacher or teacher-student, or as an 'external person', all this would have been to look at things from an inappropriate frame of reference; one which relies upon the tyranny of the paradigm case. It would be to invoke as a weapon of judgement the ideal or perfect open classroom, against which one marked off the school much as one might mark off the height of a child against a standard measuring rod.[10]

The appropriate frame of reference is quite other than one which allows of this sort of analogy. School A's point of development towards its full operation in a new school building is distinct from School B's development in ways which make it necessary to think differently about each school, even if the components of both social systems are largely similar. Perhaps what went on in School B about their open classroom programme can be applauded and what did not go on in School A can be regretted. However, it must also be realised that what went on in School B would have been inappropriate for School A at that time, rather in the way that although there is nothing wrong with Elizabethan Madrigals as such, it is inappropriate to insist that they should comprise the programme of a concert featuring a choir of children all recently arrived from a country where such music is unknown and strange.[11]

The mistake that can so easily be made is to look at schools in terms of organisation, curriculum and children's learning behaviour, leaving aside the teachers who must run the organisation, implement the curriculum and assess the learning. They are the architects of the social climate of the school, bringing to it and experiencing from it, hopes and disappointments, commitments and disengagements, rewards and punishments.

In either of School A or B there were few, if any, of what Levy calls 'chronic teachers'[12], certainly not among the staff who endured long in them. Active involvement in and subscription to a school can cost a teacher dear in social and emotional tension. It is, of course, difficult to assess this in any formal way and foolish to attempt any assessment without spending much time in the situation. So far as Team One is concerned it is possible to say that it cost the membership of one of its number, a gifted and forceful teacher who left simply because he could not accept the situation described in the first section of this chapter.[13] Neither he nor the school can be blamed. So far as the project itself was concerned it is sure that, had he been the only teacher-student in the school, his departure would have been under cover of some pretext and there would have been no-one to further spur the critical conscience of the staff towards the meeting in third term. The lack would have been serious for none of us are incapable of becoming agents of the moribund state.

But there is another side to the coin. The principal concern of the

Educational Task Force project is the understanding of the innovative process and its facilitation in schools at the hands of established professionals. That enduring core of School A's staff had been responsible for implementing a procedural change of considerable consequence and was party to the planning of a future building which would consolidate the change. If we look again at the questions from Team One which were given earlier (page 143), we can observe that they can be interpreted as suggesting in part that the new organisation did not better a more traditional one in some important respects. For example, in respect of the third question, if 'we throw too much responsibility on pupils ... in a free and open environment' it is but a step to a contention that the free and open situation *is* too demanding upon children. The question does not necessarily have this implication and it was not the implication intended by the majority of the team, who wished to suggest much the same as Mr Szorenyi-Reischl does in chapter 7, namely that a certain amount of guidance and training in using the open situation must coincide with work in it. Nevertheless, the query can be interpreted as inviting a retreat from the principle of openness and there is nothing reactionary or moribund about resisting the invitation.[14]

Further to this, the open classroom debate, or lack of it, cannot be taken in isolation from the totality of the Educational Task Force's operation. It has already been pointed out that the conflict threatened to prejudice the whole operation but that the danger was avoided. This being so, it transpired that where one avenue to this particular goal remained blocked the same goal was attainable by following another route which had been taken in the first instance to gain a somewhat different, though always related, end. Towards the end of its first year and into its second, the team's investigation of parent attitudes and involvement, described in chapter 8, gained considerable momentum and a corresponding involvement of other staff. An interview schedule was drawn up by the Educational Task Force after consultation with and guidance from various specialists in the university, presented to the staff, criticised constructively and taken back for modification by a working group consisting of the Educational Task Force and some eighteen other staff, including the principal and other senior teachers.

Inevitably the discussion included consideration of the use to which the findings would be put. Inevitably the answer included not only that the machinery of parent contact would be examined in the light of what was discovered but that the manner in which the school carried through its educational programmes would also be examined with a view to improving and demonstrating its validity, which is to say no less than that the principle of openness must be seen to withstand test. Coming from the staff as a whole more than from the Educational Task Force alone, and including a number of erstwhile opponents, this was a significant development and a very considerable gain. It bade fair to precede an addition to the brief for the team. No matter what eventuated, what was observable at this very time constituted evidence of the innovative process and the attitude compatible with it. The concept behind the Educational Task Force project was operative.

On a point of theory

Mention has been made in previous chapters of McLeish's work on attitudes and attitude formation in relation to teacher reaction to educational issues.[15] The course of the open classroom controversy in School A indicates a need for some caution about the significance of tough-mindedness and the nature of what is measured by McLeish's schedule of Radicalism. A distinction must be made between a radical attitude and subscription to a radical proposal or procedure. The staff of School A did not so much display the first as evince the second but in manner compatible with a tough-minded attitude.

It was not so easy to explain this from McLeish's analysis. As a consequence it seemed profitable to turn to the work of psychologists whose approach to attitude formation and operation was more molecular than that of Eysenck, upon whom McLeish largely relied.[16] In the view of these workers in the field of attitudes it is necessary to identify the domain of discourse, e.g. education, and then to think of attitudes and their formation in terms of that context, inferring nothing from attitudes operative in other areas which touch upon the person's life. Rather than cast the analysis in generic terms such as 'tough-minded', one now thinks in terms of latitudes of acceptance and rejection confined to a specific and precisely identified issue, say the working of *this* open classroom. The problem of many techniques for measuring attitudes, argue these psychologists, is that they tend to calculate a single score from a summation of responses upon a range of related issues. In their view this fails to take account of the fact that susceptibility to change or lack of it in respect of any one issue is not deducible from summations of this kind. This yields the conclusion that one must look within the domain of discourse itself before it is possible to explain the sort of conflict that is now under discussion. One must take note of the specific issue that it is thought worthwhile contesting; namely this open classroom.

Adopting this approach it becomes clear that the stand taken by a teacher in respect of matters concerning teaching and school organisation will largely be a product of his personal experience in schools, and will affect his judgement of whatever appears to him to be connected with school and schooling as he now experiences it. Not surprisingly, his interpretation of the behaviour of others and of what he now encounters as a teacher in association with colleagues will rank in its importance in a manner consistent with the stand taken. Whatever appears to be at odds with this stand will be resisted, and the stand itself is always characterised in specific terms.

Breer and Locke take this position a little further in their work[17]. They introduce into their discussion of attitudes the theory of positive reinforcement associated with such psychologists as B. F. Skinner. They argue that successful or unsuccessful attempts to exert personal control in a task environment such as that of a school, develops a set of beliefs, values and preferences which reflects with precision the matrix of rewards and punishments (successes and failures) experienced in that task situation. The actual beliefs, values and preferences are consonant with the preservation of what is experienced as rewarding and exclusive of what has been experienced as painful or unrewarding.

Plainly then, where a teacher brings to, or develops in, a school a set of beliefs etc. consistent with the ethos of that school, he will view as threatening to him any move which might upset the matrix of rewards obtained from working in the school. Where these rewards are precariously secured there will be an increase of anxiety over any disturbance in the situation. The teacher may appreciate the rational merits of a criticism but his almost inescapable impulse will be to resist its influence if it runs counter to the rationale of the rewarding status quo and implies an alteration – therefore a deterioration of the reward value – in the situation.

Under these circumstances the teacher will take an attitude which might be described as hard-line or conservative. But what he is hard-line or conservative about may be the unaltered preservation of a situation which is, of itself, the product of radical thinking. If by 'radical attitude' we understand an appreciation of the need for change and an absence of belief that a particular change, once made, settles the matter once and for all, then adherence to one radical *procedure* is not a guarantee of a radical *attitude*. What may happen is that people gear themselves up to commitment to one procedure which, at one point in time constitutes a radical change, pinning their hopes of reward upon taking that step. They then defend the new situation against any attack or what is perceived as an attack, namely anything that might cause a change in what has been created.

When this phenomenon involves a group of people who occupy a stable and controlling position in the social structure the situation is adequately explained by Lyman and Scott.[18] They regard man as a goal seeking, voluntaristic, intentional agent who employs, more or less consciously, strategies and tactics (games) preservative of the *status quo* they control, regarding others as allies, opponents or neutrals according to whether they seem to aid or obstruct them in this. Of society in general and the large power groups within it, Lyman and Scott remark:

With games more difficult (in a complex society) ... risk becomes a feature of everyday life ... The ability to maintain poise in the face of attempts to destroy it may become the single most important criterion in deciding the tenure of holders of power.[19]

Much the same can be said of the microcosmic as opposed to the macrocosmic; e.g. the social system of the school. Lyman and Scott also say;

(The significance of power) arises precisely from the twin facts that power always matters in social relations and that the gaining, holding, recognition, exercise and consequence of power are always problematic.[20]

It would seem fair to say that a group holding power in a precarious and uncertain situation, even when not actually under attack, will nevertheless employ that power to preclude any resistance or threat from developing and will sometimes treat something with hostility on that ground although it was not intended to be a threat. It is now a matter not of learning to live with it but of learning how to deal with it.

11. *Indications of worth*

Reception of the course

At the conclusion of their first year in School A and as teacher-students, Team One was asked to supply written comments on the course for the guidance of the director and his colleagues.

After fifteen months of working together the form of association between the people involved in the project had become a personal rather than a role determined one, that is to say that one did not regard the other principally as university lecturer, project director or teacher-student but rather as a person with whom one has a reciprocal relationship not circumscribed by the conventional niceties of position or function in the social system.[1] This materially diminishes the extent to which one must expect 'tongue in the cheek' responses to the enquiry mentioned above. When honest comments are called for one is likely to get just that kind in reply.

The team was asked to comment on the following:
The academic units of study taken at La Trobe
The Core-course
The relation between the two
The B.Ed. Task Force Course in comparison with the usual form of B.Ed.
On being placed in a school as a group
Any other aspect thought to be important

From the responses given the following digest is drawn, grouped under three heads which cover what was particularly pertinent in the replies. It is not necessary to detail each individual return since there was considerable overlap of opinion, but care has been taken to include all significant points of commendation and of criticism.

Opinions of the Educational Task Force

A. comparison with the usual form of B.Ed.

(i) I have not been attracted to the B.Ed. before because my prime interest is in the practical issues. I like the form of this course. It is far more demanding, particularly in the School A situation. This could be the basis for a greater weighting to the Core Course.

(ii) The concept of the Educational Task Force is a great improvement on the usual B.Ed. but not perfectly suited to the unit restriction of the usual form.

(iii) It is an advantage to be able to pursue two major studies during the B.Ed. course:

(a) Task Force oriented study
(b) Individual interests.

(iv) Much better than what I know of the usual B.Ed.

(v) Not sure: I would hope that we have worked on more joint or school oriented tasks than the usual B.Ed. student.

Comment The opinions expressed appear to show a confirmation of the expectations of the B.Ed. Task Force expressed in the applications to join the course. (See chapter 4.)

Remarks (i), (ii) and (v) indicate that there is a difficulty in marrying the Educational Task Force course into the usual structure of academic units and a desire for the Educational Task Force course to be an autonomous entity totally independent of the usual form of the degree.

B. *On being placed in the school as a group*

(i) A good thing – even though we were regarded with suspicion (at first). I would have liked us to have been placed more as a group in the school.

(ii) Fine. However, it does seem necessary to have more fundamental agreement on general philosophies between the members, whether it be of a conservative or radical nature, and that this position be attuned to the ethos of the school. There is the obvious rejoinder that (controversy) is beneficial as various elements come to terms with each other. It seems to me that this is outweighed by the morale destroying effect of the situation when the group is not homogenous.

(iii) The existence of the group helps considerably.

(iv) More liaison between university and school before the group arrived would have helped to clarify the group's position. While recognising the difficulties of this I feel that more definite ideas of the purpose and function of the group would have assisted early on.

(v) I find it difficult to answer this in any objective way because of the rather negative reception we as a group received.

I like being in the group. However, I feel that this has only come about since we came to work on a common task.

(vi) I think one of us was too severe in his views, though he was nearer to right than his opponents, and this could be a point to watch in the briefing of future Task Forces.

Comment. Plainly the group proved to be a mutually supporting structure under difficult circumstances.

Remark (ii) reflects a concern of the Project Director and his associates who dealt with team selection. However the difficulties and the dangers of selecting according to some criteria of compatibility are formidable. (See chapter 4.) Secondly it does appear that the team as selected succeeded in achieving an internal harmony. Remark (i) confirms, through the experience of the Educational Task Force members themselves, the error in the initial placement strategy for Team One. (See chapter 5.)

C. *Critical points*

(i) My impression is that, because of the resistance which we received in the school at the outset, the integration of theory and practice did not come about until late in the year.

(ii) I have been too rushed to get far enough away from the daily grind (school and university) to contemplate, follow up etc.
Too much was asked of us initially. I think the beginning should have been given over to the Core Course alone.

(iii) The unit system restricts depth and development although a number of the units were useful. There should be more emphasis (and credit towards the qualification) attached to the field work.

(iv) I think there should be longer units.
The units from B.Ed. seem to have been well chosen in relation to the Core Course but the brevity of courses has seriously reduced their value in relation to the Educational Task Force.

(v) Greater staff – Educational Task Force contact on problems of the school was required and more concentration of the units to the same end was necessary.

(vi) The academic units of the course have proved to be interesting but not very relevant to me as an Educational Task Force member.
There have been exceptions and I have been introduced to literature that will benefit me in time to come. However, the meaningfulness of the studies has

been limited by the amount of time I have had to really consider what I have been studying.

(vii) I feel very strongly that working on school programmes or school centred projects etc. should be given more credit in this course. The emotional demands of school are not compatible with the time that has to be spent on university assignments when the two things are separated.

(viii) I think that the Task Force might be better organised with the academic units all preceding the Task Force function and the Core Course.

Comment. The criticisms bear out the general argument of and for the B.Ed. Task Force. The more the teacher-student has his time bifurcated into discrete elements of theoretical studies and practice, the less articulation of theory and practice there is and the more the student becomes conscious of strain. This may not be true for all students of course, but, for the general advancement and improvement of practice in the schools, it does seem inevitably disadvantageous.

Some of the comments suggest that there was a simple failure to articulate the course administratively and this may well be the case. On the other hand, some other comments reflect a view that only an independent structure could fully meet the problems set out in the remarks.

The length of academic unit in relation to the expected depth of study is a problem that is not specific to the Educational Task Force. The La Trobe School of Education has considered this issue and a pattern of sequential units is emerging which will do much to diminish the force of this justified criticism.

General reflections upon the remarks as a whole

It appears fair to say that there is little outright disillusion or protest in these opinions of the first team. Criticism appears to arise within a context of realistic satisfaction. Not everything is right with the implementation of the idea but there is no clear suggestion that the idea itself is misconceived. It also appears fair to say that the discussions of the difficulties encountered in the school are informed by a balanced understanding rather than the bitterness of disappointed romanticism. From the range of remarks over the sections one can detect that there is a realisation that it takes time and skills to achieve things and that there is a distinction between tolerant tenacity and crusading insensitivity.

One of the objectives of the project was to bring about just this attitude and to impart these skills. It is an objective that is not easy of attainment under any circumstances and one which is downright unlikely to be reached by any form of teaching that is 'direct'; e.g. by lectures, discussions and so forth. The best chance of success comes through the sort of teaching that Rousseau might term to be 'negative education',[2] namely sharing the problem with the student in a joint learning venture. Remark C (viii) is a provocative one. It can be contrasted with the view in such points as C(i). As the course was arranged for Team One, its second year was comparatively light in unit load apart from the Core Course. Team members were able to audit any units offered which they felt to be of value to any of the undertakings they were engaged in but especially their work as a team on school originated tasks, towards the execution of which it was reasonable to suppose, from the remarks themselves, that they would use the knowledge gained from their first year's study. If one takes this in conjunction with the fact, confirmed again in the remarks, that it takes time to become a team in any real sense and that the process requires a task for the team to work upon before it can take effect, then the notion of preceding work as a team by study *in vacuo* does not seem attractive.

Academic progress and the Educational Task Force

Theory without practice may be insufficient for effective teacher education but the point can be reversed. There is something odd in thinking of a degree course consisting of two years practice uninformed by a disciplined body of theoretical study. If the emphasis of this book has been on the practice of the teams, it is because it has been assumed that no-one would imagine a responsible university to permit such an absurdity. However, the preface contains the advertisement for the course which details what study *was* required. As with any other candidate for the B.Ed. from La Trobe University, members of an Educational Task Force must complete nine units of study over two years. The main difference is that the Core Course represents a value of three units and is completed by gaining a half unit credit for each of six terms. Six other units are taken from the range of units open to all B.Ed. candidates, a difference here being that some units are prescribed for all of the team and are taken by the group as a whole. For Team One three units were prescribed in this way, leaving each individual the opportunity to opt for three others independently, one in the first year and two in the second. (Three *could* be taken in the second year.)

Comparison of Team One with the rest of their teacher-student year

(i) Students in the usual form of B.Ed. who enrolled at the same time as Team One took an average of 2–3 units of study over the year.

155

Each member of Team One with one exception, took 5 units of study over the year. (In this calculation the third half unit of the Core Course is not included because the team was given the vacation to complete the assignment).

(ii) The total of units taken by all other students enrolling at the same time as Team One produced forty-four per cent merit (honours) grades. Of the assignments submitted for the total of thirty-four units taken by Team One, thirty-seven per cent gained merit grades.

Of the total assignments submitted by students in any year of the B.Ed. thirty-four per cent gained merit grades.

(iii) Among all other teacher-students enrolling at the same time as Team One, twelve per cent failed to gain any merit grades at the end of the year. None of Team One failed to gain at least one merit grade.

(iv) One unit of study taken by Team One as a whole bore the title 'Curricula for Living in Cities'. Besides the seven members of the team, seven other teacher–students took this course.

The assignment work was independently marked by the three lecturers concerned in the teaching of this course and a final mark agreed by consultation and moderation of marks.

The results were as follows:

Team One: four merits and three passes.
Others taking the same course: one merit, four passes and two 're-writes' (unsatisfactory without substantial modification and extension).

Comment. Grades are not everything but they cannot be completely ignored. Taking a larger number of units in a year than the average, Team One nevertheless gained a percentage of merit marks which was not dramatically different from that obtained by students in the usual form of B.Ed. Taking students in both years of the B.Ed., when the number of units equalises out rather more – for by no means all students complete in the minimum two years – the team's percentage is slightly higher. It becomes plain that those attracted to the Educational Task Force were not academic lame ducks seeking to cloak a tendency to become giddy once in the rarified air of theory.

Specific developments in Schools A and B.

The bilingual approach. The units of study developed in connection with this work are now being tested in School B. (See Appendix 1 for an example of a unit.) As has been explained in chapter 6, this work is now a project in its own right. Eventually the service that it will offer will be utilised by numbers of schools, including School A of course.

One aspect of the Task Force project is well demonstrated by the fact. Through its teams the project can act as a vehicle for launching ideas into practical implementation at a pilot study level, after which they may well attain the status of independent projects. At this point the Educational Task Force can serve such projects in a quite different way, the team or teams acting as tools for its development. This will be further explained in a later section and still in connection with bilingual education.

Film-making in School A. As Mr Rod Nicholls mentioned in chapter 7, one of the staff of School A who took 'bit parts' in some of the films made during Team One's first year, decided to incorporate the activity into programmes of work for which he is responsible, informing what he does from the procedures and principles worked out in the first year.

The cottage alternative. Again the intention to set up an independent project which Mr Szorenyi-Reischl mentioned in chapter 8 has now been realised but in a slightly different way from the original plan which was put aside when the house became available in connection with School A. The work done over the year attracted great interest and considerable publicity. A number of schools in one area of the city were among those addressing enquiries and requests for guidance to the Educational Task Force member principally concerned with the cottage, Mr Szorenyi-Reischl or the project director. This area will now become the focus of a separate project investigating the viability of alternative forms of schooling.

Within School A itself, the hope expressed by Mr Szorenyi-Reischl for an enlargement of the cottage work has been realised. Some fifty to sixty students are involved in a larger premises and several of the staff of School A now work there in association with the Task Force member. This increase in scope makes of the 'alternative' something that is more a component part of School A's structure rather than an annexe, something essentially once removed.

It has been mentioned that the team member concerned in all this became engaged in a great deal of public discussion on the work. This is very encouraging from the point of view of teacher-student development on the one hand and from the point of view of the articulation of new knowledge with present practice on the other.

Parent contact: School A. Still in connection with the cottage, it was noticed at the beginning that migrant parents were not attracted to the idea. This is amply explained by the analysis of parent attitudes given in chapter 9. But, in the second year there was a significant increase in interest from migrant parents, explained no doubt in part by the fact that one of the teachers selected to work in the enlarged alternative is a migrant, but there is reason enough to say also that the work done by the team in meeting parents on their own ground has inspired confidence in the school and to count this fact in the explanation.

The school is now geared to conducting a thorough survey of parental attitudes and the Educational Task Force has worked long and well with a large number of staff to fashion an appropriate instrument and devise means of administering it. It is clearly the intention that the results obtained should inform the future practices of the school, although in what ways things will change remains to be seen. It would be inappropriate simply to alter school procedure to accord with parent ideas and attitudes but what is to be hoped for is that a different and more realistic machinery of parent–school dialogue will come into being, by the working of which will be achieved a mutual adjustment of view on the basis of sound and understood principles. One may make use of the dangerous term 'parent education' in this context, given that what is meant accommodates the possibility of teacher learning and precludes the influence of professional mystiques. (See chapter 9 page 121.)

Parent contact: School B. Having been charged at the outset with the responsibility of creating a structure of parent participation and parent education (in the sense just outlined), Team Two worked closely with key staff to achieve a suitable organisational plan. (See Appendix 2.)

It is all too easy to become romantic before the event, shocked by events and disillusioned afterwards. Over the next year Team Two and the staff of School B in general will test the workability of the idea. It is one thing to adopt the principle that parents should have a stake in the decision making process which determines how the school will serve the children. It is another thing to gain general parental assent to that principle and another thing yet again to bring about action based upon it.

Perhaps all that can be said at this time is that taking on the task has, of itself, oriented the team to the advance into parent territory that can break down the walls of the fortress-cum shop school. There is serious concern among the team to acquire the skills and competences necessary to this. Together with a number of staff, the team is earnestly investigating the speediest ways of acquiring a working knowledge of the language of the predominating migrant group in the area. Success in this may not bring magical results but the effort – even the intent – indicates that the teachers are adjusting to the people they serve rather than seeking to adjust the people.

The open classroom: School A. This is by way of a post-script to chapter 10. At the end of the year the school held a curriculum conference to which a number of 'outside people' were invited in the capacity of consultants in the field of diagnostic and attainment testing. By this time there was general agreement with comments such as one made by a member of staff to the effect that evaluation was needed and 'it has never really been done here'. There was no objection to the further comment, 'It could be that some assumptions we've made are not correct.

If anything more needs to be said it is this: a living idea is perhaps the most powerful thing that man can either create or encounter and it thrives on challenge and test. There is, in fact, but one way to kill it and that is to starve it to death by treating it as if it was a monument in need of protection. If the Educational Task Force had anything to do with preventing that from happening to School A's open classroom ideas then it was well done. There seems reason to suggest that the team did perform such a service.

Future possibilities

A specialist task force. The first Educational Task Forces of the project have worked to a molar plan much as in the Chicago Ford Training and Placement Scheme. The reference point has been the school and its general situation. Individual members of teams, particularly of Team One, have concerned themselves with special issues which fitted their own specialisms or interests (e.g. developing the cottage alternative while someone else on the team developed the work in film-making). Group projects were also developed and these were extremely important for the teams, but the brief for the Educational Task Force was not limited to one specific problem area.

An Educational Task Force could be employed on a molecular model; that is to say that one problem area could be identified and the team selected to tackle it and no other. It is very possible that Task Forces will be formed on this basis to serve the specific end of introducing and evaluating the approach developed by Dr Rado (chapter 6). The course constructed for them must be somewhat different from that constructed for teams to date, with work in linguistics, psycho-linguistics and language predominating, supplemented by options according to differentiation of function of team members, some taking units in sociology, others in curriculum construction and so on.

It seems likely that Educational Task Forces of this kind would have reduced membership. It is also tempting to say that one team could transfer from one school to another after, say, one year, and thus be of service to a greater number. The limited scope of operation should enable much to be done in a year of concentrated effort. But although this has its attractions it neglects the very recommendations that proved to be essential to the effectiveness of Team One. (See chapter 5 page 58.) What determines the matter is not what is to be done but what conditions of acceptance have to be established before what is done can confidently be expected to have a lasting influence; that is to say is likely to be subscribed to by the staff. And it is time that matters here.

A primary task force. Negotiations are now in train between the Victorian Education Department and La Trobe School of Education, through the Project Director, for there to be a primary Educational Task Force.

In the Australian context this development is important for a number of reasons. In training, in administration and in status, the primary school teacher in Australia, until very recently, has been separated off from his colleagues in the secondary schools (or vice-versa of course – it depends on which way you look at it). Links with the university Schools of Education have been tenuous and, on the whole, one sided. The hierarchy of qualifications has tended to emphasise the distinction between theorist ('university person') and the practitioner. The vicious result has been that 'university people' have acquired the stereotype reputation of paternalistic 'know that' lecturers. They can tell the teachers and the teachers can then go away and do. The academic is the recipe giver, never the cook, the classroom teacher is the follower never the leader, the learner, never the teacher.

As a consequence – and very understandably – the primary teacher has tended to be defensive; overtly far too submissive but covertly hostile. A sort of inverted guilt about his lack of a degree, of a respectable qualification, has manifested itself in the primary teacher's traditional suspicion of the university teacher as 'airy-fairy' but always possessed of a capability to 'argue better' and so silence or embarrass the voice of practical reason in the teacher, should he dare to tackle him.

As has been said, this is the stereotype situation. It is never precisely and so nakedly like this and no-one wants such a curious parallel to a social class war amongst those whose common concern is the furtherance of education. (At least, if anyone who counts *does* want it then it bodes ill for schooling, the teaching profession and the children of a society committed to egalitarian ideals.) But declarations of parity of esteem, even when backed by parity of material conditions, remain piously vacuous unless there is reciprocity of action and interaction between the parties.

There is not yet parity of material conditions, but, in Victoria at any rate, much is being done towards this end and one can hope that much more will be done in the future. This is to the good. It is now up to everybody concerned to implement moves towards the reciprocity of action and interaction that will complete the picture. A primary Educational Task Force is a move in that direction.

Simply because of the history so briefly touched on above it is probable that an Educational Task Force in a primary school will live through some peculiarly acute social tensions and crises. Perhaps this will again provide a problem of selection and a need for a different sort of team from one working in a secondary school. Meeting these needs may indicate something further about the general issue of teacher placement and yield further understandings of schools as social systems.

E.T.F. members as future agents of change. The Educational Task Force is a university course of advanced study which has a form compatible with the principles Getzels set out in his seminal paper to which so much reference has been made throughout this book.[3] It would therefore be quite wrong to assess the project solely in terms of the activity of teams – however many – working for circumscribed periods in particular schools. In two years the teacher-students of an Educational Task Force should gain their degrees; their secondment to the school in which they formed part of a team will be over. (Some may well ask to remain in that school but that is another matter.) There is no inconsistency in arguing that, having been placed in a team for the reason that the isolated innovator is so often reduced in effectiveness, the experience so gained will lend the individual a lasting increase in skill to take with him after leaving the formally constituted group of an Educational Task Force. Successful experience in the group, prolonged analysis, increased understanding of social systems, should all do much to make each individual a catalyst for change in whatever situation he encounters when the group is disbanded. What he has gained over two years of intensive learning is not likely to disappear with his group membership.

Of course this is conjecture and not fact at this point. A further study will be required to confirm or disprove the fact that membership of an Educational Task Force increases the likelihood that the erstwhile Educational Task Force member will continue to innovate to an extent and with an effect significantly more valuable than teacher-students who have gained the same qualification but by more usual means.

Untapped potential. The James Report in Britain envisages the creation of a training facility which is geared to the needs of schools and utilised by established professionals within them.[4] The Educational Task Force project is similarly oriented but the resource is taken to the school rather than the other way round. If one school's needs are distinct from those of another even when their situations have much in common, then any school should be able to draw upon a resource flexible enough to be incorporated within the school and to be translated into terms of that school's social system. This could be achieved by the outright institutionalisation of the Task Force idea. Were a Department of Education to budget annually so that a number of teachers equivalent to two Educational Task Forces were recruited to the B.Ed Task Force course and the teams made available to any school that wanted them on much the same terms as the two teams concerned in this account were 'engaged', then a powerful agency for educational advance would be consistently maintained and a permanent link forged between administration, university and school. Furthermore, the advance would come from a point of origination within the school. As Mackenzie points out, the notion that internal rather than external agents bring about change and advance in education is often put forward but is, in fact, far from the general case.[5] The link would be the stronger between these educational arms if such other agencies as the Department's Curriculum and Research Branch and Psychology and Guidance Service were to participate on the same terms as those people from the university concerned with the work of the Educational Task Force in the school.

The effect of this move would be to diminish any defensiveness within schools and to banish any idea that universities and similar places are imbued with a patronising zeal to better the schools in spite of the schools themselves. The brief of an Educational Task Force comes from the school and the team is part of the school. University staff do not merely counsel, inform, advise or otherwise indulge in once removed activities. They participate and suffer the consequences or reap the rewards with the rest.

In chapter 2 it was noted that something has been lost with the passing of the campus or laboratory school which was once an adjunct to institutions of teacher education. They cannot be re-instituted nor, it was argued, would it be desirable to do so even if it was possible. But the schools of the city are there and they could have Educational Task Forces. What was lost with the campus school can be replaced to the benefit both of the schools and of teacher education.

The cost will not be large. The benefits could be spectacular. It is not necessary to grant total subscription to the views of the de-schooler to recognise that there is a pessimism about schooling as it is. It is vital to the teachers that the pessimistic trend be reversed from within the schools themselves and that must have something to do with teachers and teacher education – in the schools. An administrative shift is required that suggests to teachers that the initiative and the authority of knowledge is in their hands, that they are not dancing to a tune of goals and ends that they must merely receive.[6] Yet there is little point in granting this to teachers without equipping them with the skills necessary for the job; indeed that would be to burden them with an inappropriate responsibility. Skills are less taught than learned through guided experience. They are not routine performances so much as practices intelligently adapted to particular situations. The situation is not a mere 'environment' but a social context involving people in interaction; which is precisely what is supplied to an Educational Task Force.

In a recent issue of an American journal, Allen A. Schneider remarked that the classroom teacher was one of the most under-used resources for change and improvement in education.[7] In the Australian situation at least, this is best interpeted not as indicating how little is done by teachers but as indicating how much they could do given the chance. But that, in its turn, should not be interpreted as denigrating the declared intent of more than one administration. Instead it is to say that moves such as the James Report in England, the Ford Training and Placement Programme in Chicago and the Educational Task Force project in Melbourne, have yet to be fully developed.

Final comment

This is by way of a last word rather than a formal summing up.

The Educational Task Force project has provided an absorbing insight into the workings of teacher groups and schools. In bringing it into being and directing its course, those concerned have learned alongside those who have formed the teacher-student teams and many others. One thing learned is that what one plans for and what one guards against as a result of a first experience leaves open the high probability that something different will catch one unawares next time. Having understood this, one is less likely to confuse euphoria with confidence and expectation with achievement.

In this account some things have been detailed as accomplished, particularly in the second part of the book and chiefly in respect of School A (although by no means exclusively). Other things are foreshadowed, particularly in School B. Success is not inevitable, for all that the structures set up and the preparations made as means to achieve the foreshadowed ends are no mean achievements in themselves. But the principal success has been the manner in which the teacher-students of the Educational Task Force teams have maintained and refined the process which has yielded the achievements so far secured and which permits a confident expectation that further achievements are to come.

APPENDIX 1 EXAMPLES FROM A BILINGUAL UNIT OF STUDY
(SEE CHAPTER 6)

The material given below is taken from one of the first trial units developed by Dr Marta Rado in consultation with the Curriculum and Research Branch of the Victorian Department of Education.

It is by no means the full unit and does not need to be in order to provide illustration of the approach used.

The essential of the unit is that it is amenable to relatively unambiguous translation into the dominant languages found in the schools with heavy migrant saturations.

From the unit rationale

In part, because of the magnitude of Australia's success in overseas sporting competitions in relation to her small population, the image of Australia as a land peopled by healthy rugged athletes is common in the international arena.

Sport has become an integral part of the Australian ethos. Whether sport for Australians takes the form of being a spectator or a player its importance is obvious when a hundred thousand people attend the football final or when Australians wager one thousand, eight hundred million dollars annually on horse-racing – about seventy per cent of the total annual exports of the Australian economy.

The topic was chosen firstly because it provides an initial medium to explore the Australian character and also because of the opportunities to relate to the European situation in terms of the origins of sport as we know it. Furthermore, from discussions with students newly arrived in Australia it was evident that play activities of a sporting kind were important to them.

By providing opportunities to describe pastimes in their country of origin and to sort out their impressions and develop an understanding of this aspect of Australia it is hoped the cultural shock of arriving in a new land might be cushioned for the children.

Component A. Short tapes of children describing a sample week's activities.

Introductory narration to point out that these are not necessarily typical but are provided to give some idea of the life styles of other children.

(1) John – a country boy. Working on fruit-growing property; swimming in the river; riding bicycle; school and community activities; week-end sport.

(2) Clarisa – Italian origin; inner suburban teenager.

(3) Louise and Peter – middle suburban dwellers; thirteen year old twins.

'Now that you've listened to the tapes, write down in diary form what *you* have been doing during the past week or any normal week.

Include all the activies you can remember.

Make your diary like this.

Monday
7.00   9.30

Get up Dressed Made breakfast for sisters	Washed dishes Made beds	School lessons	Lunchtime Played basketball	School lessons	Read magazines at friend's house	Helped Mum prepare dinner	Watched T.V.	Bed

'Make up a similar diary of a week in your life in (country of origin) What are the main differences between the way you lived in ****** and the way you live now?'

Component B. You may like to do a small survey of your group or class to find out;
  (1) What are the most popular forms of physical activity?
  (2) How much time is spent in playing sport?
  (3) What is the popular sport watched?
  (4) How much time do students spend watching sport?
You will need to ask at least ten students. Your table could look like this:

Students	Main physical activity	Number of hours each week	Main sport watched	Number of hours each week
Boy 1	Football	14	Football league	8
Boy 2	Soccer	10	Football league	6
Girl 1	Basketball	5	Football league	2
Girl 2	No sport played	–	No sport watched	–

NB In Australia 'football' and 'football league' are to do with Australian rules football which is quite unlike soccer or rugby.

When you have completed all the information for the table you will be able to complete the following statements.
  (a) For *most* boys in the group, the most popular sporting activity is . . .
  (b) For *most* girls in the group, the most popular sporting activity is . . .
  (c) There were . . . students who did *not* play any sport.
If you would like to find out how much time adults spend watching and playing sport, do a similar survey among your teachers.

Component C. Note to teachers. The following material contains questions which, if possible, should be treated by discussion and would be most suitable for more mature students.

Racial prejudice in sport. An Australian boy and a Greek-born boy (from School A) wrote of their experiences of racial differences at school. Their accounts follow.

Australian boy. Sport is also different to what I like. When I first came to (School A), I found the only sport being played was Soccer. So, for the first few days I just wandered around the school. Then I got the urge to accept this as the only sport and to try to learn the game. When I told the soccer boys what I wanted to do, some just laughed at the thought of an Australian boy wanting to play soccer, but what else was there to do to pass a lunchtime?

A few of the boys decided they would teach me and give me a chance. I kept getting told off for the stupid mistakes I made, but it wasn't my fault. Every time they told me to do something, they said it in Greek, and seeing that I could not understand, I just kicked the ball and I got told off. But I did make the soccer side. Now that I have started to play football (Australian rules), I was dropped just like that.

Greek-born boy. One incident that I can still recall is the time when an Australian boy wanted to try for the school soccer team. At first we all laughed at the idea and did not even bother to give him a try out. Our captain wanted to give him a chance and thought he would make the grade but we still laughed. Our captain gave him some basic lessons on soccer and with some later experience he made the grade.

    (a) Why do you think the other boys laughed at the idea of an Australian-born boy wanting to play soccer?

    (b) Would it be difficult for an Australian to learn to play soccer? (Give your reasons for your answer.)

    (c) Why do you think the Australian-born boy wanted to play soccer?

    (d) Write about any similar incident you may know about.

Analysis of unit structure

    (1) Tapes of life-styles of children.

    (2) Diaries of activities.

    (3) Geographic and other reasons determining sporting activities.

    (4) Origins – relationship to human need for fitness to survive. – development of sport as recreation from Athens and Sparta.

    (5) Why do people play sport?

    (6) Australians as 'rugged athletes'.

    (7) Surveys of other children and adults.

    (8) Which sport?

Local area – sporting venues.

Sports played in Australia and home country.

    (9) Spectator sports.

Historically treated – Olympic games; sporting festivals.

Reasons for the spectator phenomenon.

    (10) Racial prejudice and sport.

    (11) Phrases with sporting origins.

APPENDIX 1

References useful for the unit

McIntosh, P. C. *Sport in Society* (Watts, London, 1968).
Gillett, C. *All in the Game* (Penguin Books, England, 1971).
Poolard, J. *The Australian Surfrider* (Kenmore Murrey, Sydney, 1963).
Johnston, G., *The Australians* (Rigby, Australia, 1966).

APPENDIX 2 WORKING PLAN FOR A COUNCIL OF PARENTS: SCHOOL B (SEE CHAPTER 9)

To involve parents of children from forms one and two.

1. *Procedure*

   (a) Educational Task Force to visit homes of children in these forms.
   (b) Barbecue at the school for all parents visited and invited at that time.
   (c) Second visit to homes to explain further the idea of the council.
   (d) Selection of parents to be invited to form first parent groups.
   (e) Invitations extended.
   (f) Set up council: first meetings at beginning of second school term.

2. *Form of Council*

   (a) Ethno-cultural groups
      Four in number:
         Italian
         Greek
         Yugoslav
         Native Australian.
      (Careful consideration to be given to the degree to which cultural differences within one ethnic group make it difficult to form single groups under this broad classification. See Point 4 below.)
   (b) Central liaison body
         One/two parents from each group above.
         Principal
         Educational Task Force team
         Certain other staff
   (c) Meetings
      Ethno-cultural groups:
         Once monthly with one or two Educational Task Force members and certain other staff.
      Central liaison body.
         Once each term with the possibility of extra ordinary meetings.
      ('Certain other staff' will include staff with an interpreter function but will not be restricted to this instrumental purpose.)

169

3. *Functions*

  (a) Ethno-cultural groups

      (i) To discuss matters of concern and interest in respect of any aspect of school procedure and organisation.

     (ii) To secure parental involvement in contacting other parents, making community contacts, arranging parent functions in the school.

    (iii) To examine possibilities of parent group formation (regular or casual) outside school.

  (b) Central liaison body

        To make suggestions, recommendations and criticisms to be taken to the school staff meeting for discussion and report back.

4. *Concerning Ethno-cultural groups*

Rotation of membership as a means of allowing a maximum number of parents to participate tends to produce short lived groups without a real inter-active base. It was therefore decided to constitute new groups from time to time to allow of a desirable incidence of participation without the undesirable effect of rotating membership within one group.

Notes pp. 1—11

CHAPTER 1

1 Department of Education and Science, *Teacher Education and Training* (James Report) (H.M.S.O., 1972) p. 75.

2 *Ibid.* p. 12.

3 'That education has an important part to play in social change is undoubted, but its influence is secondary and not primary ... When the aim changes the education changes but the aims have to change first.' Ottaway, K. C., *Education and Society* (Routledge and Kegan Paul, London, 1953).

4 Perry, L. R., 'What is an Educational Situation?' in Archambault, R. D. (ed), *Philosophical Analysis and Education* (Routledge and Kegan Paul, London, 1965).

5 McLeish, J., *Students' Attitudes and College Environments* (Cambridge Institute of Education, Cambridge, 1970) p. 3.

6 Farley, R. *Secondary Modern Discipline* (Adam and Charles Black, 1960) p. 11.

7 James Report. p. 12.

8 *Ibid.* p. 13.

9 *Ibid.* p. 18.

10 See Strauss, A. L., *Mirrors and Masks* (The Sociology Press, San Francisco, 1967) pp. 103–9.

11 Sarason, S. B., 'Towards a Psychology of Change and Innovation', *American Psychologist*, 22, 1967. See also Claydon, L. F. and Lovegrove M. L., 'Course Construction and Student Participation', *Journal of Curriculum Studies*, vol. 4, no. I, May, 1972.

12 Schools Council Working Paper 27, *Cross'd with Adversity* (Evans/Methuen, London, 1970).

13 Work done in the Liverpool Educational Priority Area provides a good example. See the Liverpool E.P.A. Occasional Papers published by the Liverpool E.P.A. In America examples are afforded by the 'Head Start' projects.

14 See Langford, G., *Philosophy and Education* (Macmillan, London, 1968) p. 7.

15 'The Relation of Theory to Practice In Education' originally published in the *Third Yearbook of the National Society for the Scientific Study of Education*, Part I (University of Chicago Press, 1904). Also quoted in Wirth, A., *John Dewey as Educator* (Wiley, N.Y., 1966) chapter 5.

16 Dewey, J., *Democracy and Education* (Macmillan Paperback, London, 1961) pp. 328ff.

17 Peters, R. S., *Ethics and Education* (Allen and Unwin, London, 1966).

18 Illich, I., *Deschooling Society* (Harper Row, N.Y., 1970) and Goodman, P., *Growing Up Absurd* (Random House, N.Y., 1956).

171

19 See Central Advisory Council for Education (England), *Children and Their Primary Schools* (H.M.S.O., 1967) and U.S. Department of Health, Education and Welfare, *Programmes for the Educationally Disadvantaged*, Office of Education Bulletin no. 17, 1968.

CHAPTER 2
1 Wirth, A., *John Dewey as Educator.*
2 Getzels, J. W., 'Education for the Inner City: A Practical Proposal by an Impractical Theorist', *School Review*, vol. 75, no. 3, Autumn, 1967, pp. 283–99.
3 *Ibid.* p. 294.
4 *Ibid.* p. 295.
5 James Report, p. 34.
6 Getzels, 'Education for the Inner City', p. 291.
7 Cited in, Schwartz, H., 'A Social Systems Approach to Training Teachers for Urban Schools: The Ford Training and Placement Program', in *Education at Chicago*, Autumn, 1971, Department and Graduate School of Education, University of Chicago.
8 *Ibid.* p. 14.
9 See *Resource Papers, Ford Training & Placement Program, April 1970*, University of Chicago and Chicago Board of Education.
10 Schwartz, H. and Doyle, W. 'The Practicability of a Theoretical Model' in *Resource Papers F.T.P.P. April, 1970*, p. 21.
11 Hannam, C., Smyth, P. and Stephenson, N., *Young Teachers and Reluctant Learners* (Penguin Books, London, 1971).
12 Tribute is due to the then Head of the Education Department of the College, Mrs E. B. Tidy, O.B.E., for her encouragement and assistance in this work, which did not at all fit in with the established way of doing things at that time.
13 Plowden Report, *Children and Their Primary Schools* (Central Advisory Council for Education, H.M.S.O., 1967).
14 Sarason, 'Towards a Psychology of Change'.
15 Miller, H. L. (Ed), *Education for the Disadvantaged* (Free Press, N.Y., 1967). Chapter 3 repeats criticisms of this kind in respect of a number of projects in America.
16 Allport, G. W., *The Person in Psychology* (Beacon Press, Boston, 1968) p. 19.
17 The following is drawn from Riles, W. C. (Chairman), *The Urban Education Task Force Report* (Praeger, N.Y., 1970). 'It may be possible to learn as much about . . . success from studying . . . intent and execution . . . as from analysing the quantitative relationships between program components and summary measures.'

CHAPTER 3
1 Tsounis, M. P., 'Improving the Processes of Settlement for Migrants in Australia'. Unpublished paper given at the consultation called by the organisation, Australian Frontier, and held at Melbourne University in May, 1972. In Australia the two terms 'migrant' and 'immigrant' are interchangeable.
2 See 'Australian Immigration: Consolidated Statistics No. 4', Immigration Department, Canberra, 1970.

3 See Rainwater, L., *Behind Ghetto Walls* (Penguin, London, 1972).

4 Tsounis, 'Improving the Process of Settlement in Migrants in Australia'.

5 'The aim of courses in General Studies should be to provide stimulus to the student, an incentive to self education and an attitude of critical awareness.' 'Teacher Education and Training' (James Report).

6 Fantini, M. D. and Young, M.A., *Designing Education for Tomorrow's Cities* (Holt, Rinehart and Winston, N.Y., 1970) p. 13.

7 Considerable elaboration and modification to this statement is required and provided in chapter 6 by Dr Rado.

CHAPTER 4

1 From Claydon, L. F., *City Educational Task Force*, Address to the Conference of the Board of Inspectors of Secondary Schools at Monash University, November, 1971. Distributed by the Victorian Department of Education; also held by National Library, Canberra.

2 Getzels, 'Education for the Inner City'.

3 See Sharrock, A., *Home School Relations* (Macmillan, 1970) pp. 12ff. Liddle, G. P. and Rockwell, R. E., *The Role of Parents and Family Life* in Webster, S. W. (Ed), *Educating the Disadvantaged Learner*, Part III (Chandler, San Francisco, 1966).

4 Eysenck, H. J., 'General Social Attitudes', *Journal Social Psychology*, *19, 1944*, and *The Structure of Human Personality* (Methuen, London, 1953).

5 McLeish, J., *Students' Attitudes & College Environment* (Cambridge Institute of Education, Cambridge, 1970).

6 *Ibid.* p. 43.

7 *Ibid.* p. 51.

8 *Ibid.* p. 52.

9 *Ibid.* Appendix IV, pp. 228, 234, 235. It was clear that we could not expect to undertake a study of anything like the range of McLeish's work. It was a matter of making a selection on good grounds.

10 *Ibid.* p. 110.

11 *Ibid.* p. 116.

12 *Ibid.* p. 117.

13 *Ibid.* p. 118.

14 A seminar on the Educational Task Force was held by Victorian Institute for Educational Research on 7 June 1972. The speakers were L. F. Claydon, M. Rado and N. Szorenyi-Reischl plus two members of the first Educational Task Force.

15 The advertisement appeared on 24 and 29 June. A cartoon in the Melbourne newspaper *The Age* of 30 June depicted a member of university staff crouched behind a barricade and armed with a rifle and bayonet. He addresses a young man beyond the barricade who carries hand-grenades and other weapons. The caption reads, 'Have you ever considered an academic career at La Trobe?' The following appeared in the national newspaper, *The Australian*, 1 July 1972: 'This year has grown the Americanisation of student politics, seen most clearly at Melbourne's youngest university, La Trobe, where a group has been accused of running a terror campaign aimed at staff and students.'

16

	Tough-mindedness	Formalism	Radicalism
School A	3–12	2–11	67–91
Team One	1–7	3–10	69–80
School B	2–15	2–16	61–88
Team Two	1–15	1–18	78–84
Maximum possible	23	25	100

CHAPTER 5

1 See chapter 2, p. 24.

2 There is agitation for this: see for example 'E.P.A. Task Forces Now!' in *Priority News*, No. 2, May, 1972, published by the Liverpool E.P.A. project in England.

3 The paper reflects the new found confidence in its frankness of approach. The opening paragraphs include the following: 'At an earlier staff meeting H.N. outlined some of the activities of the Task Force. He reminded us of the essence of the Task Force concept as Leslie Claydon and others, including the Principal, saw it when it was set up . . . The central theme was that this group would work in consultation with the staff on problems identified by the staff or by Task Force members.

For various reasons this close professional consultation has not, to date, taken place. Reasons for this are well known but to ensure that we are all now thinking along these lines let us outline some of them.' The paper ends with a series of proposals for group activities for the staff to discuss and to approve or otherwise.

4 Doyle, W. J., 'The Ford Training and Placement Program: A Summary of Major Impressions', Internal Paper: Graduate School of Education, University of Chicago, 1970.

5 Some idea of the range of units may be gained from the titles given below:
Cultural diversity and the Migrant Contribution
Curricula for Living in Cities
Home–school Relations
Language Use and Language Users
Education in a time of Social and Moral Reconstruction
Social Class and Language Utilisation

6 Ginsberg, H., *The Myth of the Deprived Child* (Prentice Hall Inc., N.Y., 1972) p. 234.

7 Fantini, M. and Weinstein, G., *Making Urban Schools Work* (Holt, Rinehart and Winston, 1968) p. 6.

8 Getzels, 'Education for the Inner City'.

9 Kohl, H., *The Open Classroom* (Methuen, London, 1970) p. 27.

INTRODUCTORY COMMENTS TO PART 2

1 In Part 3, chapter 10.

2 Getzels, 'Education for the Inner City'.

3 Report of the Central Advisory Council for Education (England) *Half Our Future* H.M.S.O., 1963).

4 See Cochrane, D. B. and Major, A. J., 'Education and Relevance: A Philosophical Analysis of William Glasser', *Journal of Educational Thought*, vol. 6, no. 2, 1972.

5 Fantini and Weinstein, *Making Urban Schools*, p. 6.

6 It was pointed out in chapter 4 that the brief for the first team was put together after the dialogue between staff and team which occurred before the team went into the school. This part of the brief constructed was the least well defined in the discussions, probably because there was some division of opinion within the staff and between staff and team about its importance.

CHAPTER 6

1 Kunz, E. I., *Refugees and Eastern Europeans in Australia* in Price, C. A. (Ed), *Australian Immigration: A Bibliography and Digest*, no. 2, 1970, A.N.U., 1971 p. A 46.

2 *Ibid.* p. A 17.

3 Lynch, P., 'Australia's Immigration Policy' in Roberts, H. (Ed), *Australia's Immigration Policy* (University of Western Australia Press, Perth, 1972) p. 10.

4 *Migrant Education Survey, 1970*, Curriculum and Research Branch Research Project, Victorian Education Department, 1970.

5 Johnston, R., *Future Australians, Immigrant Children in Perth, Western Australia* (A.N.U., Canberra, 1972) p. 3.

6 Price, *Australian Immigration*, p. A 39.

7 Ongoing.

8 Martin, J. I., 'Migrants: Equality and Ideology', Fifth Meredith Memorial Lecture in the Series One. Delivered at La Trobe University, 26 April 1972.

9 Lynch, P., *Immigration in the Seventies* (Government, Printer, Canberra, 1971) p. 16.

10 In Federal Government's Response to Book 4 of the Report of the Royal Commission on Bilingualism and Biculturalism, a document tabled by the Canadian Prime Minister on 8 October 1971.

11 Martin, J. I. *Community and Identity* (Australian National University Press, Canberra, 1972) p. 126.

12 Gaarder, A. B., 'Organization of the Bilingual School', *Journal of Social issues*, 23, 1967.

13 Clyne, M. G., *Perspectives on Language Contact* (The Hawthorn Press, Melbourne, 1972) and *Transference and Triggering* (Martinus Nijhoff, The Hague, 1967).

14 The Project now being separately funded to operate in a number of schools.

CHAPTER 7

1 Rod Nicholls was a tutor in the Media Centre at La Trobe University before taking up his present post. He has worked professionally in films and television in Britain and the United States. He worked for a year with B.B.C. personnel attached to the British Open University.

2 Kael, P., *I Lost it at the Movies* (Little, Brown and Co. Boston, 1965).

3 McLuhan, M. H., *The Mechanical Bride; Folklore of Industrial Man* (Vanguard, Toronto, 1951).

4 Eliot, T. S., 'East Coker' in *Four Quartets* (Faber and Faber, London, 1959).

5 Peck, R. E., 'Films, T.V. and Tennis' in Robinson, W. R. (Ed), *Man and the Movies* (Penguin, Baltimore, 1969).

6 Welles, Orson, quoted in Noble, P., *The Fabulous Orson Welles* (Hutchinson, London, 1956).

7 Steinbeck, J., *Once There Was A War* (Corgi, Transworld, London, 1961).

8 Choppra, P., 'The I Hate School Syndrome', paper presented to the Australian Psychological Society in Brisbane, 1968. Quoted in Roper, T., *The Myth of Equality* (Heinemann, 1971).

9 Poignard, J. and Mann, F., 'Curtain of Illusion – The Odyssey of The Children's Caravan', *School Library Journal*, N.Y., Febuary, 1971.

10 Vernon, M.D., *The Psychology of Perception* (Penguin, London 1962).

11 Wiseman, S., *Education and Environment* (Manchester University Press, 1964) p. 24.

12 Hawkins, D., 'Messing About in Science', *Science and Children*, February 1965. Quoted in Holt, J., *How Children Learn* (Penguin, London, 1970) p. 141.

13 *Ibid.*

14 Gagné, R. M., *The Conditions of Learning* (Holt, Rinehart and Winston, San Francisco, 1965.

15 Cudlipp, H., 'The Mass Communications Jungle' *U.K. Press Gazette*, no. 101, August 1968.

16 Balázs, B., *Theory of the Film* (Roy, New York 1953).

17 McLuhan, M. H., *Counterblast* (Rapp and Whiting, London, 1970).

18 Grierson, J. (Ed Hardy), *Grierson on Documentary* (Faber and Faber, London, 1966).

19 Gance, A., quoted in Dickson, T., *A Discovery of Cinema* (O.U.P., London, 1971).

20 Hilgard, E. R., *Theories of Learning* (2nd Edition) (Appleton-Century-Crofts, N.Y., 1956).

21 Fantini, M. D. and Young, M. A., *Designing Education for Tomorrow's Cities* (Holt, Rinehart and Winston, N.Y. 1970).

22 *Ibid.*

23 Holt, *How Children Learn*, p. 50.

24 Murray, J. C., 'Film Teaching at the Crossroads' in, *'Idiom'*, *Journal of the Victorian Association for the Teaching of English*, March, 1971.

25 Holt, *How Children Learn*.

26 Choppra, 'The I hate School Syndrome'.

27 Fantini and Young, *Designing Education for Tomorrow's Cities*.

28 Gagné, *The Conditions of Learning*.

29 Doenau, S. J., *Sit still, Listen and Be Quiet* (Wass and Co., Epping, 1970).

30 In Gagné, R. M. (Ed) *Learning and Individual Differences* (Charles Merrill, Columbus, 1967).

31 Beard, R., *Teaching and Learning in Higher Education* (Penguin, London, 1970).

32 Cruikshank, A. and Leonard, T., *The Identification and analysis of perceived*

problems of teachers in inner-city schools, Occasional Paper No. 1. (National Institute for Advanced Study in Teaching Disadvantaged Youth, 1967).

33 Beer, D., *The Community School*, 52nd Handbook (National Society for the Study of Education, Chicago, 1953).

34 Hood, S., *A Survey of Television* (Heinemann, London, 1969).

35 McLuhan, *Counterblast*.

36 *Ibid.*

37 Jennings, R. G., 'Inner Suburban Schools' in *The Education Magazine*, March, 1972. Victorian Education Department, Melbourne.

CHAPTER 8

1 Goodman, P., *Compulsory Miseducation* (1971), Henry, J., *Essays on Education* (1971), Reimer, E., *School is Dead: An Essay on Alternatives in Education* (1971), Postman, N. and Weingartner, C., *Teaching as a Subversive Activity* (1971), Kohl, H., *36 Children* (1972), all Penguin Books.

2 Goodman, *Compulsory Miseducation* (Penguin, 1971). Dennison, G., *The Lives of Children* Vintage Books. Fromm, E., *The Sane Society* (Rinehart, N.Y., 1955).

3 It seems to me that the community school movement, although owing a lot to 'progressive' educational thought, differs from it in so far as the child's personal development is not taken in isolation but within the social and physical realities of the actual environment.

4 This lack of support is explained by the results of the investigation subsequently carried out by the task force team on parent attitudes. See chapter 8.

5 Providing a link with another aspect of the Educational Task Force project in the school. See chapter 7.

6 It is known that children frequently settle for jobs on the basis of some fantasy about its nature of the nature of its rewards.

7 Tolerance of the delayed responsibility incurred by serving an apprenticeship places demands upon personal stability which are often far more important than skill, ability and intellectual competence in determining whether the youngster wins through to tradesman status.

8 In a term paper written at the close of the first year the Educational Task Force member working in the cottage put the case as follows. 'Our interest was with the 13–15 year olds. Teacher discussions generally indicate that this is the group where the greatest problems can be anticipated. It is also the period in which the child makes or has made some key decisions for his future. Will he stay on at school or not? If he leaves what sort of occupation will he enter? For those who stay at school, choices of specialisation must be made. These however are the choices as usually perceived by adults. The issues which seem significant to the child in these years tend to be quite different ... The significant issue for the adolescent is the establishing of a secure role for himself in a new world of relationships with adults and peers, having moved from a position of dependence within the family and society to a point where he feels physically and sexually equal.

Against this background how realistic is the usual school experience? The tradition of school subjects will not only appear irrelevant to the student; they may actually be irrelevant to his needs at this time. This is not to claim that, at some future time, they may not regain their importance (but at this time) the classroom teacher finds his relationship cannot be maintained by a physical dominance (and) because of the felt lack of relevance of his subject matter by the students, neither can it be rested at this stage upon his expertise with the discipline.

9 School B had a native Australian minority also. Much the same characteristics of low attainment and troubled backgrounds were observable in respect of this group. One is uneasily aware of the 'poor white' syndrome which is so well documented from America. Again the multicultural approach seems to be of vital importance.

10 One may notice how this sort of conclusion helped to inspire the work described in chapter 8 of this book.

11 There were indeed a number of very responsible newspaper reports upon the Educational Task Force project which included mention of the cottage. These include reports by Iola Hack in *The Age*, Elisabeth Synhausen in *The Bulletin* and Tom Roper in *The Review*.

CHAPTER 9

1 See Jackson, B. and Marsden, D., *Education and the Working Class* (Routledge and Kegan Paul, London, 1962).

2 See chapter 5 p. 60.

3 It was envisaged from the beginning that the team would participate in the construction of the core course after the first term. At times this produced headaches for the project director; it never produced 'easy options' for those taking the course.

4 Hannam, Smyth and Stephenson, *Young Teachers and Reluctant Learners.*

5 Midwinter, E. *Social Environment and the Urban School* (Ward Lock Educational, London, 1971).

6 Goffman, E., *The Presentation of Self in Everyday Life* (Penguin Books, London, 1969) p. 55.

7 See McGeeney, P., *Parents Are Welcome* (Longman, Green and Co., London, 1969).

8 Goodacre, E., *School and Home* (N.F.E.R., London, 1970) p. 51.

9 See, Musgrave, F. and Taylor, P. M., *Society and The Teacher's Role* (Routledge and Kegan Paul, London, 1969).

10 Midwinter, *Social Environment and the Urban School.*

11 McGeeney, *Parents are Welcome.*

12 That in-principle issues always underpin educational change of any magnitude explains why the Educational Task Force course included academic units of a philosophical nature such as 'Education in a Time of Social and Moral Reconstruction'.

13 Central Advisory Council, *Children and Their Primary Schools.*

14 Hannan, Smyth and Stephenson, *Young Teachers and Reluctant Learners.*

15 Bryson, L. and Thompson, F., *An Australian New Town* (Penguin Books, London, 1972) p. 10.

16 McLeish, *Students Attitudes and College Environments.*

17

Maximum score	Tough-mindedness 25		Formalism 25		Radicalism 100	
	Mean	S.D.	Mean	S.D.	Mean	S.D.
Parents	14.3	5.68	14.9	4.3	69.5	7.8
Teacher group E.T.F.	11.1	5.1	10.4	4.05	71.3	8.8
Applicants	6.4	3.86	6.0	3.84	77.2	7.6
School A	5.6	4.9	5.0	3.7	80.2	7.2
School B	8.9	3.86	9.9	4.63	74.9	6.92

18 By McLeish the formalistic person responds affirmatively to the proposition that: 'Mark lists, when made public, spur children on to greater effort.' He responds negatively to:
'Children should be allowed to help each other with their school work in class'
and
'Work in school should be arranged entirely on an individual basis.'
This was the predominating pattern of response in the parent group tested.

19 Goodacre, *School and Home.*

20 'Southern European families are very much aware of the value of education... They have come from countries where a rigid class structure makes education the only way up for their children. If they cannot afford (it), or, if when educated, they cannot find a patron to ease the child's way into advantageous employment, then the family must resign itself to one more generation of poverty.'
From Clemens, A., 'Immigration: Italian Style' in *The Migrant Child and the School*, Papers by the Migrant Study and Workshop Group, Psychology and Guidance Branch (Education Department of Victoria, 1972) p. 15.
The predominant migrant group in School A was not Italian but, as the passage indicates, the situation described is not confined to Italy.

21 Bryson, and Thompson, *An Australian New Town.*

22 Stephen Thernstrom makes the point in connection with American society: a stable working class may be achieved in the absence of any upward occupational mobility and at a level of subsistence which is considerably lower than that 'calculated (as necessary) by middle-class investigators'. Thernstrom, S., 'Poverty in Historical Perspective' in Moynihan, D. (Ed), *On Understanding Poverty* (Basic Books, N.Y., 1968).

23 After one interview with a mother in distress, with the daughter interpreting, the latter turned upon her mother, spat in her face and lamented bitterly that she was cursed with such a burden. The mother sat, dumb with misery, the child was in an agony of ambivalence.

24 See chapter 5 p. 62.

25 It is a matter of debate as to whether teachers should be differently trained to fulfil an extended role or whether the staff of a school should carry special personnel with functions other than teaching, as in many American schools.

26 See p. 129.

27 See chapter 5, p. 61.

28 One may point out, for example, that no proposal to investigate alternative styles of schooling procedures featured in the brief for Team Two. This is not an omission in some standard pattern that must be followed.

CHAPTER 10

1 See chapter 1, p. 13.
2 Getzels, 'Education for the Inner City'.
3 Ginsberg, *The Myth of the Deprived Child.*
4 Getzels, 'Education For the Inner City.'
5 The number is not atypical. In School B, for example, there was a ninety per cent turn-over of staff in one year.
6 One of the team later wrote that it was as if the rest of the staff had come to see the team as plastic surgeons and had discovered in themselves no need for plastic surgery.
7 Ginsberg. *The Myth of the Deprived Child.*
8 Shortly after the second time the Educational Task Force sought to bring such considerations before the staff an article in the journal of the teachers' organisation to which most High School teachers belong raised very similar queries about open classrooms. Barnes, R., 'What Should Happen in an Open Classroom?' in *The Secondary Teacher*, August, 1972.
9 Bremer, J. *et al*, *School Without Walls* Holt, Rinehart and Winston, N.Y., 1972).
10 The paradigm is, of course, a construct and not a reality. The theoretical model is all too frequently recommended by comparing it with the worst of actual examples of the 'traditional' classroom.
11 See chapter 3, p. 38.
12 Levy, G., *Ghetto School* (Pegasus, N.Y., 1970).
13 He was transferred to the usual form of B.Ed. course and so was not lost to the ranks of the teacher-student.
14 The ambiguity of the situation was recognised by the Educational Task Force. In a paper one of its number wrote: 'In regarding the open classroom as an innovation in need of evaluation the Task Force have found themselves in a paradoxical position. Entering the school *as* innovators they found themselves designated as the opinion leaders of the laggards, so casting them in the role of conservatives who wished a return to the status quo.'
15 Especially in chapter 4.
16 Sherif, C. W. and M, and Nebergall, R., *Attitude & Attitude Change* (W. B. Saunders and Co., Phil., 1965).
17 Breer, P. E. and Locke, E. A. *Task Experience as a Source of Attitudes* (Dorsey Press, 1965).
18 Lyman, S. M. and Scott, M. B., *A Sociology of the Absurd* (Appleton Century Crofts, N.Y., 1970).
19 *Ibid.* p. 211.
20 *Ibid.* p. 213.

CHAPTER 11

1 See Claydon, L. F., 'What is Involved in Knowing One's Pupils?'. Paper delivered

to the Conference of the Australasian Philosophy of Education Society in Christchurch, New Zealand, August, 1972. Copies available from Dr L. Brown, School of Education, University of Sydney N.S.W.

2 See Claydon, L. F. (Ed), *Rousseau* (Collier Macmillan, London, 1969) p. 66.

3 Getzels, 'Education for the Inner City'.

4 James Report.

5 Mackenzie, G., 'Curricular Change ...' in Miles, M. (Ed), *Innovations in Education* (Teachers College, Columbia, N.Y., 1964).

6 See Claydon, L. F., 'Teaching and Commitment to Value' in *Educational Philosophy and Theory*, vol. 5, no. 1 March, 1973.

7 Schneider, A. A., Editorial in *The Journal of Teacher Education*, vol. XII, no. 2, Summer, 1972.

Further reading: a limited bibliography

Community, home and school

Auerbach, A. B., *Parents Learn Through Discussion* (Wiley, N. Y., 1968).
Miller, G. W., *Educational Opportunity and the Home* (Longman, London, 1971).
Poster, C., *The School and the Community* (Macmillan, London, 1971).

Film

Robker, L., *Elements of Film* (Harcourt, Brace and World, N.Y. 1968).
Smallman, K., *Creative Film Making* (Collier, N.Y. and London, 1969).

Language and education

Carroll, J. B., *Language and Thought* (Prentice Hall, N.Y., 1964).
De Cecco, J. P. (ed), *The Psychology of Language, Thought and Instruction* (Holt, Rinehart and Winston, N.Y., 1967).
Lawton, D., *Social Class, Language and Education* (Routledge and Kegan Paul, London, 1969).

Migrants and their education

Allway, D. and Cordasco, F., *Minorities and the American City* (David McKay, N.Y. 1970).
Cordasco, F., *Italians in the United States* (Oriole Editions, N.Y. 1972).
Deutsch, M., Katz, I. and Jensen, A., *Social Class, Race and Psychological Development* (Holt, Rinehart and Winston, N.Y., 1968).
Morrish, I., *The Background of Immigrant Children* (Allen and Unwin, London, 1971).
Patterson, S., *Dark Strangers* (Penguin Books, 1965).

Schools and schooling procedures

Goslin, D. A., *The School in Contemporary Society* (Scott Foresman, Ill., 1965).
Hertling, J. E. and Getz, H. G., *Education for the Middle School Years: Readings.* (Scott Foresman, Ill. 1971).
Kohl, L. R., *The Open Classroom* (Methuen, N.Y., 1970).
Richmond, K., *The School Curriculum* (Methuen, London, 1971).
Mays, J., Quine, W. and Pickett, K., *School of Tomorrow* (Longmans, London, 1968).
Schaefer, R. J., *The School as a Center of Inquiry*, (Harper and Row, N.Y., 1965).

FURTHER READING: A LIMITED BIBLIOGRAPHY

Teachers and teacher preparation

Tuckman, B. W. and O'Brian, J. L., *Preparing to Teach the Disadvantaged* (Free Press, N.Y., 1969).

Silberman, C. E., *Crisis in the Classroom* (Vintage Books, N.Y., 1971).

Strom, R. D., *The Inner-city Classroom* (Charles Merrill, Columbus, Ohio, 1965).

Teaching and the disadvantaged

Brickman, W. W. and Lehrer, S. (ed), *Education and the Many Faces of the Disadvantaged* (Wiley, N.Y., 1972).

Goldstein, B., Steinberg, B., and Bredheimer, H. C., *Low Income Youth in Urban Areas* (Holt, Rinehart and Winston, N.Y., 1967).

Passow, A. H. (ed), *Education in Depressed Areas*, (Teachers College, Columbia University, N.Y., 1960).

Passow, A. H. (ed), *Deprivation and Disadvantage* (U.N.E.S.C.O., Hamburg, 1970).

White, W. F., *Tactics for Teaching the Disadvantaged* (McGraw Hill, N.Y., 1971).

The Australian context

Connell, W. *et al.*, Growing Up in an Australian City (A.C.E.R., Melbourne, 1966).

Fensham, P., *Rights and Equality in Australian Education* (Cheshire, Melbourne, 1970).

Henderson, R. F. *et al.*, *People in Poverty; A Melbourne Study* (Cheshire, Melbourne, 1970).

Stevenson, A., Martin, E. and O'Neill, J., *High Living: A Study of Family Life in Flats* (Melbourne University Press, 1967).

Taft, R., *From Stranger to Citizen* (University Western Australia Press, 1960).

Zubozycki, J., *Immigrants in Australia* (Melbourne University Press, 1960).

The social systems approach

Corwin, R. G., 'Strategies for Organizational Innovation: An Empirical Comparison', *American Sociological Review*, vol. 37 no. 4., August, 1972.

McCampbell, J. F., *A Transactional Style of Organizational Process*, F.T.P.P. News Brief (University Chicago Ford Training and Placement Program, 1972).

Index